Weath
at Sea

Third Edition

David Houghton

fernhurst
B O O K S

Produced in consultation with the RYA

First published 1986 by Fernhurst Books,
Duke's Path, High Street, Arundel,
West Sussex, BN18 9AJ, UK
Tel: 01903 882277 Fax: 01903 882715

New Editions 1991 and 1998

Write, phone or fax the publisher for a free,
full-colour brochure.

Printed in Hong Kong

British Library Cataloguing in Publication Data:
A catalogue record for this book is available
from the British Library.

ISBN 1 898660 49 2

Acknowledgements

Thanks are due to Bill Anderson and Alison
Noyce of the RYA for their helpful comments
on the manuscript.

The publishers gratefully acknowledge
permission to reproduce the following
photgraphs:
Photographs by R. K. Pilsbury I.S.O., F.R.P.S.
except for:
University of Dundee: pages 10, 11, 20(top),
30, 31, 45.
State University of New York: page 59.
Dartcom: page 61.

Cover design by Simon Balley.

Design and DTP by Creative Byte

Contents

1   Introducing weather   4

2   Introducing weather maps   8

3   The wind on the deck   14

4   The message of the clouds   17

5   The life of a depression   24

6   Weather information – sources and definitions   32

7   DIY – Your own observations   37

8   Weather maps and bulletins – how to use them   39

9   Weather hazards   42

10   Winds near coasts   47

11   Afternoon winds and sea breezes   50

12   Winds over the open ocean   54

13   Waves, swell, wind and tide   56

14   Tropical cyclones   59

15   Mariner's weather lore   61

16   Practical examples   63

Appendix 1   Coriolis force   66

Appendix 2   The thermal wind   67

Appendix 3   DIY – Your own weather map   70

Appendix 4   UK sea areas   79

Index   80

1 Introducing weather

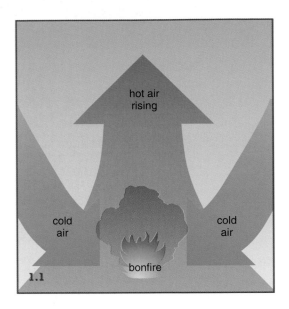

1.1

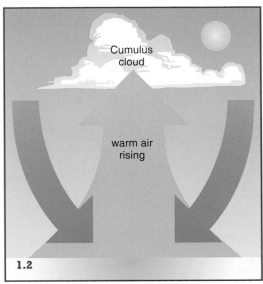

1.2

When we talk about weather we think of everything going on in the atmosphere around us: its temperature, which affects our comfort; its humidity, which determines how far we can see through it; its cloudiness and whether it is raining; and in particular the speed and direction in which it is moving, the wind, which determines where and how fast we can sail. This book is concerned with real weather – the wind in **your** sails and the clouds in **your** sky – in the Northern Hemisphere. The only skill you need is the ability to construct a jig-saw: fitting together all the pieces of evidence available to get the best possible picture of the wind and weather you are about to experience on the water.

WHAT DRIVES IT

The driving force for all weather activity is heat from the sun. It works rather like a garden bonfire. The air over the fire is heated and rises, carrying smoke with it, and is replaced by colder air moving in from the sides (figure 1.1). So it is with the weather. Corresponding to the fire we have land or sea warmed by the sun, the temperature rise depending on the colour and character of the surface. Black tarmac gets a lot hotter than a green field, a desert hotter than a

forest or an ocean. There is very little direct heating of the air by the sun.

So warmed air rising in one area is offset by cooler sinking air somewhere else. A good illustration of cooled air sinking is a chest freezer. Open the lid and the cold air, far from rising, stays put in the chest. On the world scale, air heated by the sun in the tropics rises and is replaced by cooled air moving in from the polar regions (figure 1.3). On a local scale we have, for example, sea breezes, when air warmed over land rises to be replaced by cooler air moving in from the sea (figure 11.2); or cumulus clouds which are evidence of bubbles of rising air and the invisible air movements replacing them (figure 1.2). In all cases there is a compensating movement of air aloft.

WATER IN THE AIR

Everywhere there is some water vapour in the air: in dry air only a little, in humid air a lot. Cloud and fog are suspensions in the air of billions of tiny droplets of water or ice crystals. Water is continually evaporating from oceans, lakes and moist ground, and this evaporation absorbs heat energy. If you hold a wet finger in

Small cumulus.

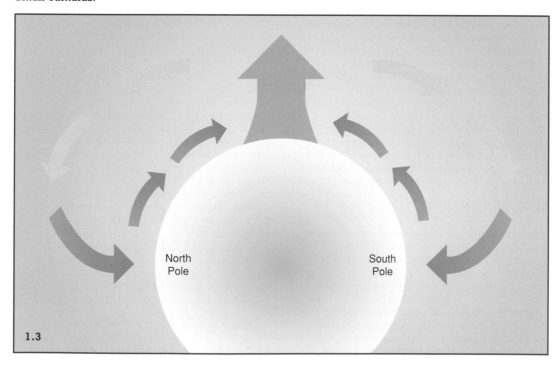

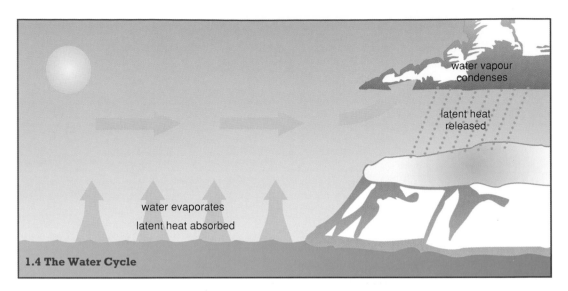

1.4 The Water Cycle

the wind it feels cold because the process of vaporising the water takes heat out of your finger. The temperature of an open swimming pool will drop 2 or 3 degrees every day because of evaporation. Heat from the sun may make up for some of the loss during the day, but covering it to stop the evaporation will make an even greater difference.

Once in the air the water vapour is carried around the world, and wherever it condenses into water droplets the same heat energy that was used in evaporation is released back into the atmosphere (figure 1.4). This is why it is called *latent heat* (hidden heat), the heat stored as it were in the water vapour. So water is responsible for much of the active weather we experience because it moves heat energy around in vast quantities. Thunderstorms and tropical cyclones derive most of their energy directly from the release of latent heat through condensation. So it really is very important. In fact wherever you have rain you are likely to find stronger winds because of the extra energy available from the release of latent heat.

AIR MASSES

There should be no mystique about air masses. Precise definitions belong only to the geography textbook. All the sailor needs to know is the common sense approach. How cold or warm the air is and how wet or dry depend on where it has come from. For instance, air from the Arctic carried on a cold northerly wind will be both cold and dry, requiring appropriate clothing and skin care. Air from over a sub–tropical ocean will be warm and damp.

Keeping dry may be difficult, and the more serious problem of sea fog must be considered (see chapter 9). You cannot rely on the local wind direction to track down the source of the air – it may have come by a roundabout route. You will normally need to refer to recent weather maps to find out.

THE WORLD'S MAJOR WIND PATTERNS

The world's major wind systems are more complicated than the very simple model in figure 1.3 for two main reasons. Firstly the very uneven distribution of land and sea, deserts and forests, which causes some areas to become much hotter or colder than others, even in similar latitudes; and mountains which simply get in the way. Secondly, the deflection due to the earth's rotation. In consequence the simple cell of figure 1.3 breaks into two or more cells. The largest, most persistent and easily recognised of these cells incorporates the trade winds: air rising over the tropics being fed by the northeast and southeast trades which originate in a broad zone of subsiding (sinking) air in the horse latitudes (figure 1.5), home of the large subtropical anticyclones. Further north and south, roughly from latitudes 35 to 70 degrees we have winds from a generally westerly point but with many eddies, small and large, with air rising in some and subsiding in others. Then in polar regions the air is generally subsiding and feeding cold air equatorwards.

WEATHER SYSTEMS

An instantaneous picture of what is going on in

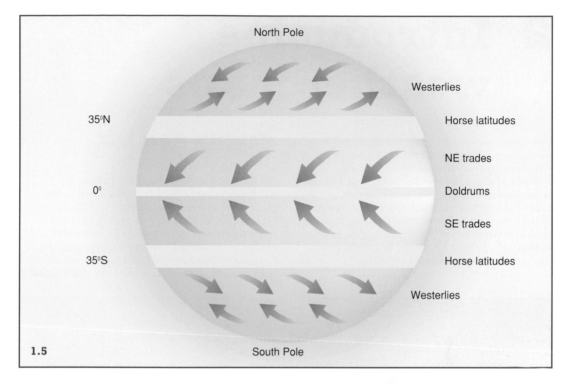

North Pole

Westerlies

35°N   Horse latitudes

NE trades

0°   Doldrums

SE trades

35°S   Horse latitudes

Westerlies

1.5   South Pole

the atmosphere is available from weather satellites which show the clouds acting like dye in the air mapping out the weather systems. The eddies in the westerlies are particularly interesting. If you could somehow see all of the air from the satellite, and if it was instataneously "frozen" and the clouds removed, you would see a whole landscape of mountains, hollows, ridges, valleys and cols around the globe, overlaid by two or three vast meandering rivers. Unfreeze the air and let it move again and you would see the air in the hollows and mountains circulating around the centres in opposite directions: hence the name cyclone (low) and anticyclone (high). In a newly formed cyclone the spiralling motion would be shallow, extending upwards only 1000 metres or so, and moving downstream steered by the 'river' of air overlying it. Typically too this is where the river is likely to be narrow and fast flowing, hence its name jet stream. An older cyclone would be much deeper, some 10,000 to 15,000 metres, with the main flow following a large meander around it.

WHY WEATHER?

If you were able to fill the air with a tracer which revealed not only its horizontal movements but also the up and down ones you would see a gradual descent of air in the anticyclones and a generally faster but very uneven ascent in the cyclones. It is this ascent and descent which really makes 'weather' – the variety of cloud, rain, sunshine and showers changing by the day and hour. Rising air cools, causing cloud to form and then rain – the sort of weather you experience in a cyclone. Subsiding (descending) air warms, so the cloud disperses and the weather is fine – the sort of weather you experience in an anticyclone. The speeds are almost too slow to measure directly: often no more than a few metres per day. But in cumulonimbus clouds and tropical cyclones upward speeds are locally much higher, perhaps as much as 60 knots.

To understand why rising air cools and subsiding air warms think of a tyre. Undo the valve, let the air out and the temperature of the valve will drop towards freezing because the air is expanding. Pump up the tyre and the valve will become too hot to touch because the air is being compressed. A refrigerator works on this principle. Where the working gas is being compressed the pipes get hot, where the gas is expanding it gets cold. In the atmosphere wherever air is rising it is moving into lower pressure aloft, so it expands and cools. Wherever it is subsiding it is moving into higher pressure, so it is compressed and warms.

2 Introducing weather maps

The traditional weather map has for over 100 years been accepted as the best way of charting the winds over an area, as well as saying something about the weather. And its language is international: a graphical presentation of the wind and weather in terms of isobars (lines of equal pressure) and fronts (boundaries between cold and warm air masses). Weather maps are published by many countries, and everywhere the graphics have the same meaning.

MAPPING WEATHER SYSTEMS

In Chapter 1 we suggested that if the air suddenly became visible from a satellite the world's weather systems would look like a typical hilly landscape. We would see what looked like mountains and hollows, valleys and ridges. A topographic map and a weather map have many features in common. On a weather map instead of contours – lines of equal height

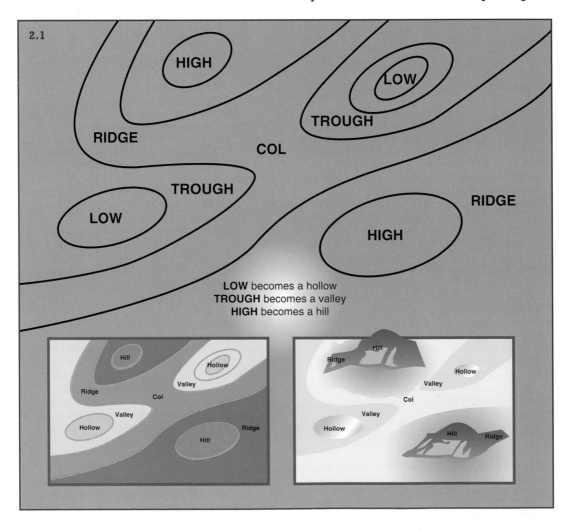

2.1

LOW becomes a hollow
TROUGH becomes a valley
HIGH becomes a hill

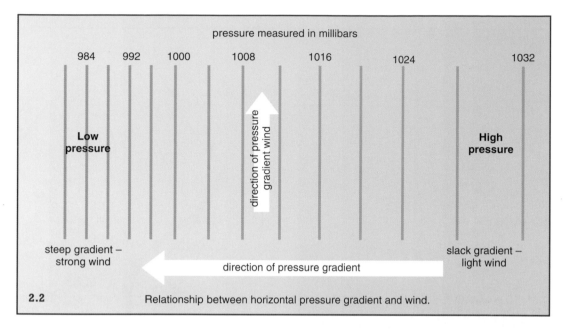

2.2 Relationship between horizontal pressure gradient and wind.

above sea level – we have *isobars* – lines of equal weight at sea level. Mapped out by the isobars (figure 2.1) we have areas of high pressure – *highs or anticyclones* – corresponding to mountains; areas of low pressure – *lows, depressions or cyclones* – corresponding to hollows; *troughs* of low pressure equating to valleys; and *ridges* and *cols* which have the same names. With contours of height, the closer they are together the stronger (steeper) the gradient. So with isobars: the closer they are the stronger the gradient of pressure.

The units used for atmospheric pressure are *millibars* or *hectopascals*, depending on the country you are in. They are interchangeable. 1000 millibars is the same as 1000 hectopascals. You will see from the dial of your barometer that values of pressure are normally between about 970 and 1040 millibars. The deepest low ever recorded in temperate latitudes was 913 millibars, near Iceland. Anticyclones rarely exceed 1050 millibars. You may still come across pressure readings in inches of mercury, dating back to the early barometers where the weight of the atmosphere was balanced against a column of mercury.

THE GRADIENT WIND

What makes the weather map especially useful is the direct relationship between the difference in pressure between any two points – the pressure gradient – and the wind; hence the name *gradient wind*. The stronger the pressure

gradient the stronger the wind.

If the earth did not rotate the wind would blow directly from high to low pressure, as you would expect. However, because the earth is rotating all the winds appear to be deflected. The deflecting force is known as *Coriolis Force* and it varies with latitude; the nearer you are to the axis of rotation, i.e. the higher the latitude, the stronger it is. Near the Equator the Coriolis force is zero and winds do blow directly from high to low pressure. Everywhere else the Coriolis force bends the wind, to the right in the Northern Hemisphere and to the left in the Southern Hemisphere, until a balance is achieved between the pressure gradient force and the Coriolis force. The Trade Winds are a good example of the Coriolis effect. Air moving south towards the equator is deflected to the west, giving us the Northeast Trades (figure 1.5). Northward moving air in the Southern Hemisphere is similarly deflected giving us the Southeast Trades.

You don't have to understand Coriolis Force to appreciate and interpret a weather map. If you want a more detailed explanation turn to Appendix 1. But all you need to know here is that, except near the equator, the gradient wind blows parallel to the isobars with a strength proportional to their distance apart (figure 2.2). Closely spaced isobars indicate a strong pressure gradient and strong winds, and widely spaced isobars indicate a weak pressure gradient and light winds. Also because the Coriolis Force depends on the latitude so does the relationship

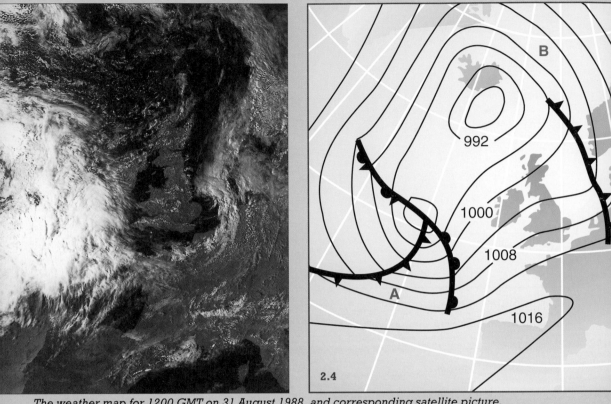

The weather map for 1200 GMT on 31 August 1988, and corresponding satellite picture.

between the pressure gradient and the wind: the lower the latitude the stronger the wind for a given spacing of isobars (see figure 2.3 opposite). The direction of the wind deflection due to Coriolis force is best remembered by Buys Ballot's Law (see figure 2.7).

The gradient wind is a real wind and is experienced at a height of about 500 metres, i.e. above the influence of surface friction. You can observe it when low clouds are present. But, you may protest, the gradient wind is measured on the weather map from sea level isobars, so how can it be the same as the wind at 500 metres up? Strictly speaking it is not quite the same, but there is normally little difference; and friction makes such a mess of the wind lower down that, over land, the 500 metre wind is the nearest you can get to the sea level gradient wind.

MEASURING GRADIENT WIND DIRECTION

The direction of the gradient wind is given by the orientation of the isobars on the weather map. Practice taking a compass bearing on the movement of the low clouds, and compare it with the run of isobars at your position on the latest weather map. This way you will bring the weather map alive.

Remember that wind direction is always the direction from which the wind is coming; in contrast to current which is the direction to which the water is flowing. The gradient wind direction at point A of fig. 2.4 is due west, at B it is southeast. For definitions of the points of the compass turn to Chapter 6.

MEASURING GRADIENT WIND SPEED

Figure 2.3 is a universal scale for obtaining the speed of the gradient wind from a weather map. (Meteorologists call it the 'geostrophic' meaning 'earth–turning' scale.) Measure the distance apart of adjacent isobars. Set your dividers to the same distance on the distance scale of figure 2.3 and transfer this distance to the wind scale at the appropriate latitude. The scale is for isobars

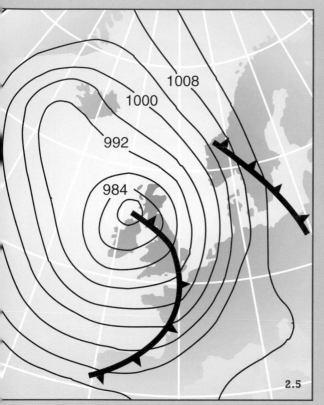

1008

1000

992

984

2.5

The weather map and satellite picture for 24 hours later.

Universal scale for obtaining wind speed in knots from a weather map with isobars at 4 millibar intervals

Step 1: Measure the distance apart of adjacent isobars on any weather map for the area you want. If no distance scale is provided use the relationship between distance and latitude: 1 degree of latitude equals 60 nautical miles.

Step 2: On the scale below, set your dividers to the distance you measured in Step 1. In this case 100 miles at 50 degrees N.

Step 3: Transfer your dividers with the setting obtained in Step 2 to the 'geostrophic' wind scale on the right, again for the appropriate latitude. Interpolating between the two vertical lines gives a wind speed of 32 knots.

Step 1

Step 1

low

50°N

100 miles

Step 2

SCALE OF NAUTICAL MILES

100 200 300 400 500 600 700

70°							70°
60°							60°
50°							50°
40°							40°

100 200 300 400 500 600 700

Step 3   GEOSTROPHIC WIND SCALE
IN KNOTS FOR 4 MB INTERVALS

80 25   10

70°			70°
60°			60°
50°			50°
40°			40°

0 40 25   15   10

2.3

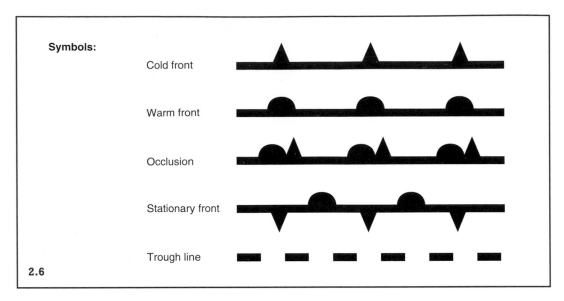

Symbols:

Cold front

Warm front

Occlusion

Stationary front

Trough line

2.6

at intervals of 4 millibars. If the intervals on the weather map are different you must multiply the speed appropriately – eg. by 8/4 if the spacing is 8 millibars, 5/4 if it is 5 millibars. Make sure you get the latitude right. The same spacing of isobars gives a 25 knot wind in the Clyde and over 40 knots off Malta.

WEATHER AND WEATHER SYSTEMS

The relationship between weather systems and the weather is not so clearly defined as with isobars and wind, but it is worth summarising the main features. Highs and the ridges extending from them are typically areas where the air is gradually subsiding and the clouds tend to disperse giving relatively fine weather. Lows and their attendant troughs are characterised by rising air, cloud and rain. The ascent of air is often very uneven and much of it is concentrated in the troughs where the cloud is thickest and the rain heaviest, often with relatively bright weather either side. The heat energy which is released as the rain falls contributes to stronger winds in the troughs.

Figures 2.4 and 2.5 are two weather maps 24 hours apart showing a deepening low pressure system approaching the British Isles from the west and turning north towards Scotland. The corresponding satellite pictures are also shown. You will find it interesting to compare the two, noting in particular the relatively clear weather in the ridge and where the pressure is high, and the masses of cloud associated with the low and its fronts. The more you look at weather maps

and their corresponding satellite pictures the more you will realise that while it is useful to think in terms of typical weather associated with highs, lows, troughs, ridges and fronts, they vary greatly in detail. In fact no two depressions, or any other weather systems, are ever identical, not in 1000 years.

FRONTS

One particular sort of trough is a front, a boundary between air masses of different characteristics. If the advancing air is relatively warm it is a *warm front*, if cold, a *cold front*. The symbols used on the weather map are shown in figure 2.6. A front is always found in a trough of low pressure, but the majority of troughs are not fronts. The special characteristics of fronts are easy to understand and the sequence of different types of cloud fascinating to follow as they go by. They are described in detail in Chapter 5.

USING WEATHER MAPS

A weather map is sometimes known as a *synoptic chart*, i.e. a presentation of weather at a particular time. A single weather map tells what is happening at the time of the map. A sequence of weather maps, typically at intervals of 12 or 24 hours, provides a broader picture and help you tune in to the 'mood' of the weather.
A shipping bulletin will always mean much more if you have a recent weather map in front of you. Chapter 6 tells you where to get one, Chapter 8 how to get the most out of it. Putting your own observation into the frame will help towards a sense of reality – see Chapter 7.

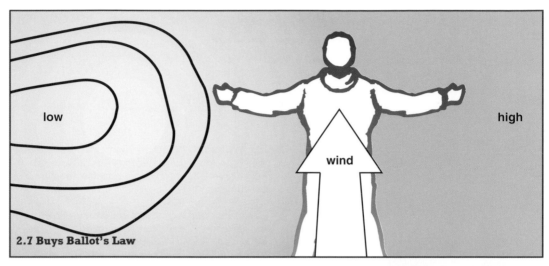

2.7 Buys Ballot's Law

WEATHER MAP WORDS

Most of the terms used in connection with weather maps have now been introduced.
In summary:
An area of low pressure has any of three names – *low, depression, cyclone*
An area of high pressure has one of two names – *high, anticyclone*
A *ridge of high pressure* is an extension of a high and is often found between lows
A *trough of low pressure* is an extension of a low
A *cold front* is the leading edge of advancing cold air
A *warm front* is the leading edge of advancing warm air
An *occlusion* is a front, cold or warm, resulting from a cold front overtaking a warm front and pushing all the warm air up above the surface (see Chapter 5)
An *isobar* is a line joining points having the same pressure
The *pressure gradient wind, or gradient wind,* is the wind measured from the weather map

BUYS BALLOT'S LAW

This is a simple rule (figure 2.7) for use when thinking about weather maps and highs and lows; in particular when you want to relate your own wind observation to the map. It states:
If you stand with your back to the wind the lower pressure will be to your left hand in the northern hemisphere.

BACK AND VEER

Back and veer are defined in relation to the clock (figure 2.8).

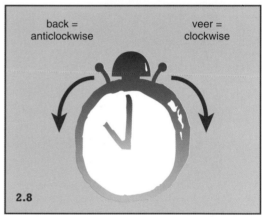

back = anticlockwise   veer = clockwise

2.8

Veer is a clockwise change in wind direction
Back is against the clock

WHAT WEATHER MAPS DO NOT TELL US

Weather maps do not tell us everything about the wind on the deck.
Weather maps do not tell us anything about:
• the influence of showers on the wind
• sea and land breezes,
  and how they may develop
• the influence of coasts and
  islands on the wind
• the influence of water or
  land temperature on the wind
• the influence of wind on the waves and what happens when there is a tide running

There is a lot to work out for yourself. It is not difficult, in fact it's fun and Chapters 3, 4, 11, 12 and 13 tell you how.

3 The wind on the deck

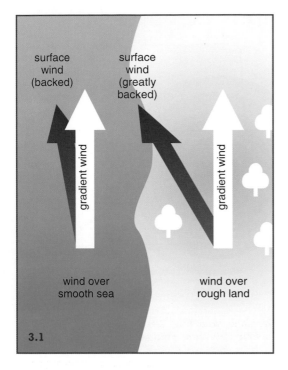

surface wind (backed)

surface wind (greatly backed)

gradient wind

gradient wind

wind over smooth sea

wind over rough land

3.1

Down at deck level surface friction, or drag, upsets the balance between the pressure gradient and Coriolis forces. It reduces the wind speed, as you would expect, and it also makes it blow towards low pressure. The greater the drag the greater the reduction in speed and the greater the bend. Figure 3.1 shows the sort of difference from gradient wind to expect on land and sea. Even larger differences will sometimes be experienced over land, especially at night, as we will see below.

This means that if you are moored in a landlocked harbour, or at home, you should not expect the wind at deck level to tell you much about the wind on the nearby water. The movement of low clouds will be much more useful, as will of course the shipping forecast. It is well worthwhile practising looking at low clouds. Take a compass bearing on their movement and subtract 15 degrees to get the wind direction on the water. Make a note in your

log. With a little practice you can also judge the wind speed on the water in terms of Beaufort Force (see Chapter 6) from how fast the clouds are moving.

The ability of the gradient wind to get down to the surface depends critically on how well the air at deck level is mixing with the air higher up. When the wind is strong there is plenty of turbulence and the effect of drag is minimised. At lower wind speeds the stability of the air becomes very important, influencing not only wind speed and direction, but also visibility and cloud type.

STABILITY AND INSTABILITY

The words *stable* and *unstable* describe how buoyant the air is, that is how easily it rises or sinks:

> air which is warmer than the air around rises – it is *unstable*
> air which is colder than the air around sinks, or stays put if it is already near the ground – it is *stable*

The stability of the air has a profound effect on:
- the wind at deck level and its gustiness
- the visibility
- the clouds (see also Chapter 4)
- the characteristics of the wind blowing off the land (see Chapter 10)

In unstable conditions:
- the wind is relatively strong – around 90% of the gradient wind – because the air is continually overturning, the air aloft bringing its wind down with it to replace air which has been slowed by friction
- the wind is gusty because of this overturning
- the visibility is good because the air is well mixed
- clouds are lumpy, of the cumulus type

In stable conditions:
- the air at deck level is relatively light, and may stop moving altogether
- the visibility is poor and fog is likely
- clouds are layered – stratus type

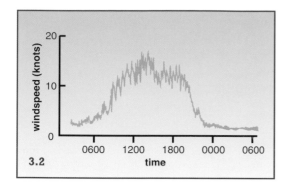

3.2

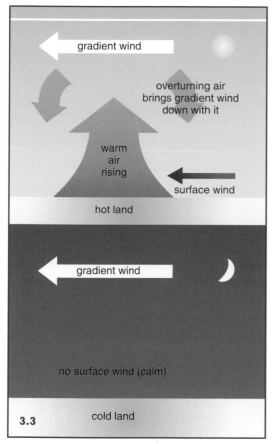

3.3

or no cloud the ground cools rapidly, cools the air near it making it stable and the wind quickly dies. Sailing near the coast you are likely to experience these land temperature effects on the wind whenever the gradient wind is offshore.

A variation in wind through the day may also occur at sea, but the small rise in water temperature due to the sun is often masked by changes in water temperature as the tide ebbs and floods or near river estuaries – river water and sea water often have very different temperatures. The warmer the surface, land or sea, the stronger the wind is likely to be.

One commonly overlooked influence on the wind at sea is the varying temperature of the top of low cloud. If the cloud persists day and night the sea temperature may stay the same – no sun to warm it, or clear sky to let it cool – but the top of the cloud will warm by day and cool at night (figure 3.4) making the wind at sea a few knots stronger in the early hours than in the afternoon.

WEIGHT OF WIND

This is related to the stability of the air. Variations in wind speed between the foot and top of the mast can cause a difference of up to 50% or more in the heeling moment on the boat for the same measured wind speed. If, for instance, your wind reference is a masthead anemometer, the wind at deck level and the heeling moment will be less in stable air than in unstable. If your wind reference is what you feel on your cheek at the helm you may be surprised by the heeling experienced in stable air because of the stronger wind at the top of the mast.

TO PREDICT THE WIND ON YOUR DECK

- read the speed and direction of the gradient wind from the latest actual and forecast weather maps and interpolate to give the wind 'now' – Chapters 2 and 8
- confirm by looking at any low clouds
- consider how the gradient wind may be modified by surface friction and stability of the air
- compare your ideas with the latest forecast for your area (Chapters 6 and 8)
- consider modifications due to coastal effects (Chapter 10) and sea or land breezes (Chapter 11)
- add changes forecast

Over land there is a 24–hour cycle in the stability of the air which is responsible for a very marked 24–hour cycle in wind strength (figure 3.2). As the sun rises it heats the ground and thus the air near it (figure 3.3). This air becomes increasingly unstable and as it rises it is replaced by colder air from aloft bringing more and more of the gradient wind down with it until the wind reaches a maximum in mid–afternoon. As the sun goes down the temperature falls and the wind decreases. After dusk, if there is little

Wind dying as the land cools: altocumulus above.

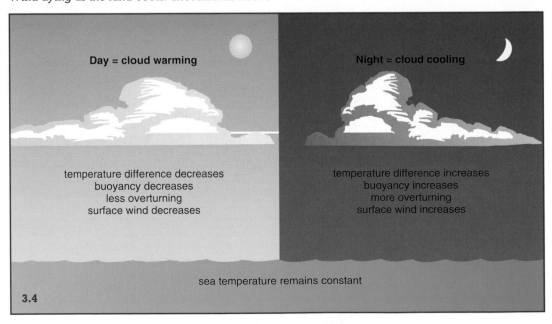

Day = cloud warming

temperature difference decreases
buoyancy decreases
less overturning
surface wind decreases

Night = cloud cooling

temperature difference increases
buoyancy increases
more overturning
surface wind increases

sea temperature remains constant

3.4

Altocumulus and altostratus at sunset. The colour of the cloud depends on how it is illuminated.

Clouds show up a great variety of events in the atmosphere, some of them involving changes in the wind. On pictures taken from satellites above the earth, the clouds map out the large-scale weather systems, particularly the depressions with their attendant troughs and fronts, and suggest many and varied smaller-scale wind movements down to the limits of resolution of the pictures (about two miles).

Looked at from below, the clouds are just as meaningful. The sequence of clouds ahead of a typical warm front tells of the advance of the warm front and perhaps its depression as well (see Chapter 5). But the majority of cloud messages relate to events on a much smaller scale, a mere few hundred metres or so. Cumulus clouds, for instance, tell of pockets of rising air which are replaced by air moving downwards in between the clouds.
Every cloud has a message of some sort. The sailor needs to recognise features which relate to the character of the wind or to changes in the general weather picture which herald major changes in wind speed and direction. In general the message of the high clouds is about events far aloft or at least several hours ahead, while low clouds provide evidence of wind changes from minutes to two or three hours ahead. We must also try to rule out signs which are unimportant or capable of misleading.

COLOURED CLOUDS

The colour of a cloud depends on how it is illuminated. If the sun is shining on it the cloud will appear white; if the sun is behind it, it will appear dark. If it is illuminated at a glancing angle when the sun is rising or setting it will be beautifully coloured. The colour will change as the cloud moves across the sky or as the sun moves over the sky. This change in colour normally has no significance where the wind is concerned, except for that enshrined in the well-known adage 'red sky in the morning, shepherd's warning; red sky at night shepherd's delight'. This saying is well founded. The most colourful skies at sunrise are when high clouds are increasing from the west and illuminated at a glancing angle by the sun – and we know

Cirrus aloft, small cumulus below.

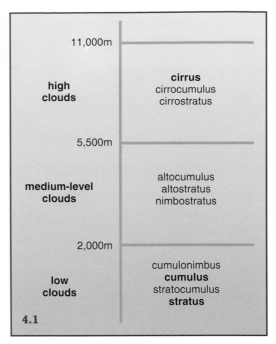

11,000m	
high clouds	**cirrus** cirrocumulus cirrostratus
5,500m	
medium-level clouds	altocumulus altostratus nimbostratus
2,000m	
low clouds	cumulonimbus **cumulus** stratocumulus **stratus**

4.1

Altocumulus.

that high clouds increasing from the west are characteristic of an advancing depression and bad weather to come. Conversely, clouds breaking up from the west are often the last evidence of a trough moving away to the east, and illuminated by the setting sun. These too appear beautifully coloured. The bad weather has gone by, and is likely to be followed by a ridge of high pressure.

THE NAMES OF THE CLOUDS

Clouds are named and classified according to their height and shape (see photographs and figure 4.1). Flat clouds are defined by the word *stratus* (meaning 'layer') or the prefix *strato-*. Lumpy or heaped clouds are described by the word *cumulus* (meaning 'heap') or the prefix *cumulo-*. Feathery clouds high in the

atmosphere are known as cirrus (meaning 'tuft' or 'curl') and the prefix *cirro-* is used to describe other high clouds and *alto-* is used to describe other clouds in the middle levels of the atmosphere. The words *stratus* and *cumulus* on their own identify clouds whose base is below 2000m. *Stratoculumus* is a layer of low cloud which has lumpy or roll features. *Nimbus* is used to describe a raining cloud. *Cumulus* may be combined with *nimbus* to give *cumulonimbus* – heaped rain cloud. A layer cloud from which rain is falling is *nimbostratus*.

FLAT CLOUDS

Flat clouds are characteristic of stable air. They often possess some shape or structure but this is usually due to warming or cooling of the top of the cloud and must not be interpreted in terms of any wind pattern at the surface. However a large and distinctive feature appearing in a layer of cloud may be significant.

A line or band of low cloud, or thicker cloud within a cloud layer, may indicate a change in wind speed or direction or both. If the line or band is stationary it may be due to local convergence of airstreams caused by a feature of the nearby land or a significant change in water temperature over the sea. If the line is moving it is clearly a feature of the air mass and a small windshift (normally a veer) is likely as it passes by. Think of these features in the

Stratocumulus.

atmosphere as small–scale replicas of the weather–map systems: an advancing line of cloud can be thought of as a very minor trough giving a small and probably temporary veer in the wind direction as it goes by.

If there is little or no wind an approaching line of stratocumulus cloud is likely to herald wind from a direction to the left of the line of advance; in other words the line of advance indicates the direction of an increasing gradient wind with the surface wind some 20 degrees to the left of it. However the approach of a bank of very low stratus or fog may herald less wind because fog is often a feature of very stable air where vertical mixing is inhibited and the effect of friction becomes more pronounced. If the wind is light to start with the increased influence of friction on arrival of the fog may bring it to a complete halt.

There are very many variations on the theme of lines and bands of cloud, and it is important to realise that the atmosphere is never completely uniform over an area, even over a smooth sea. There are always variations and it is not easy, even for a meteorologist, to distinguish between those lines of cloud that suggest a wind change at the surface and those that do not.

LUMPY CLOUDS

Lumpy or cumulus clouds are characteristic of unstable air. They are found most frequently over land in the afternoon when the temperature is at maximum, when pockets of air heated at the

ground rise until the cooling due to expansion brings their temperature back to that of the surrounding air.

Look for a moment at a single cumulus cloud (figure 4.2). If it is stationary, that is if there is no gradient wind, air will rise from the heated surface into the cloud to be replaced by air moving down (subsiding) around the outside of the cloud, creating a very simple circulation pattern. The wind strength in the inflow area is indicated by the size of the cloud. For a small cloud, say 100 metres across and 300 metres in vertical extent, it will be less than a knot; but for

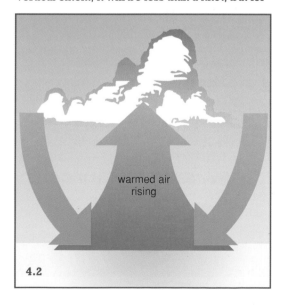

warmed air rising

4.2

Satellite picture showing cumulus clouds of varying sizes over relatively warm land, some arranged in rows. Wind WNW.

Fair-weather cumulus.

Towering cumulus; hard edges indicate turrets pushing upwards – showers are likely.

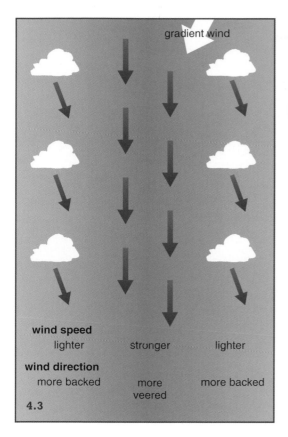

gradient wind

wind speed
lighter   stronger   lighter

wind direction
more backed   more   more backed
                   veered
4.3

Cumulus in a single cloud street – typically downwind of a hill or hot spot such as an airfield.

a towering cumulus cloud of the order of 500 metres across and up to 5000 metres high it may be 15 or more knots.

In practice there is usually some pressure gradient wind, and the convergence of air into a small cloud is a relatively minor detail superimposed on the main wind.

CLOUD STREETS

Over the sea cumulus clouds are often found in regularly spaced lines. The best examples of these are in the trade winds where they extend for hundreds of miles. Cloud streets show up a regular pattern in the vertical movement of air which is like a horizontal roll. Between the lines of cloud you will find the stronger, more gusty and slightly veered winds, and beneath the lines of cloud somewhat lighter and more backed winds (figure 4.3).

Sometimes near land you may notice a single cloud street, that is a single line of cumulus clouds down–wind of something that is producing them – a hot spot, a hill or an island. Once produced, the cumulus clouds are carried away in a line stretching downwind for many miles and the pattern of lighter and backed wind under the street, and stronger and usually veered wind either side of it, will also persist.

RAINING CLOUDS

So far we have considered fair–weather clouds, or at least clouds where there is no sign of any rain falling. Rain makes a fundamental difference to the wind characteristics of a cumulus cloud. The main reason for this is that the first rain to fall out of the base of the cloud evaporates into the air beneath and cools it, often by several degrees. This cooled air descends and the more it is cooled the more rapidly it descends. Thus instead of air rising into a cloud we have not only rain falling out of the cloud, but air as well. The drier the air beneath the cloud the more it is capable of being cooled by evaporation, and so long as there is enough rain coming out of the cloud the colder the air becomes. The cooled air literally drops out from beneath the cloud with the rain and spreads out in all directions at the surface. The light wind which was moving in towards the cloud suddenly becomes a squall rushing out and away from it (figure 4.4).

There is always plenty of visual evidence of this change. You can see the rain falling, often in grey streaks below the cloud, sometimes in a dramatic arch of black cloud spreading out from the parent cloud. The squall is necessarily short–lived because there is only a limited amount of air below the cloud to be cooled by evaporation of rain into it. Once the squall has passed the rain usually continues for a while, some ten to twenty minutes for a typical shower cloud before it is exhausted. The wind coming

Cumulonimbus and shower

out of the cloud gradually dies away with the rain.

The larger shower clouds, however, keep going for longer, and while rain falls from one part of the cloud, air continues to be drawn upwards into another part. The name 'cumulonimbus' is sometimes reserved for these big clouds. A large thunderstorm cumulonimbus may last for an hour or more – sometimes for up to four hours.

Usually there is a pressure gradient wind, but often the squall from a reasonably sized shower cloud will temporarily override the pressure gradient wind, and will augment it where they are both in the same direction.

CLOUD BANDS

There are many different types of cloud band and they form for a wide variety of reasons. Most of them tell us something about the wind. Examples are bands of thicker (or thinner) cloud within a layer of cloud in stable air, lines of cumulus cloud, cloud streets and so on. A band of cloud may be observed lying along the coast, layered cloud if the air is stable or cumulus cloud if the air is unstable. If the coast is fairly flat this band is likely to indicate a convergence of airstreams (figure 10.2). A hilly (and

particularly a mountainous) coast will frequently appear cloudy simply because the air has to rise over the high ground.

An approaching band of towering cumulus clouds is usually associated with a trough of low pressure, quite a frequent occurrence in an unstable air mass. The intensity of the trough can vary greatly; the cloud and rain may pass in ten minutes or take several hours. On a satellite picture a minor trough is seen as a fairly narrow band of cumulus cloud. On a weather chart the plotted observations will show falling pressure ahead of the trough and rising pressure behind it, maybe no more than 2 or 3 millibars down and up for a minor trough, with stations situated near the line of the trough reporting a shower. In terms of wind a back of 5 to 10 degrees might be observed over a distance of 5 to 30 miles ahead of the trough, and a veer of about the same amount as it passes.

Some of the most interesting features are the long bands of high cloud stretching from horizon to horizon with high–level winds blowing along them, sometimes at high speeds – maybe as much as 200 knots. Such clouds can be very useful predictors (see photograph p69). If the band of high cloud is stationary the weather is unlikely to change in the next twelve hours or so. If the band is the forward edge of increasing

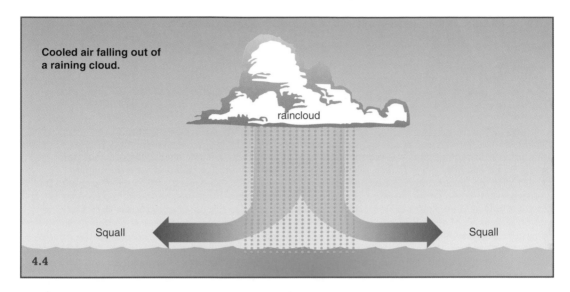

Cooled air falling out of a raining cloud.

raincloud

Squall

Squall

4.4

or thickening high cloud it tells of an advancing trough, usually a front, and its associated depression. Conversely, if the high cloud is moving away and the sky clearing it suggests that the trough has passed and better weather is on the way. These observations can be further supported by noting, if possible, the direction of movement of high cloud. If the wind aloft in an advancing area of high cloud is markedly veered on the surface wind (usually 90 degrees or more) it is a certain sign of an approaching trough, usually a warm front. Conversely, observations of the high cloud associated with a cold front which has just passed reveal upper winds which are markedly backed on the surface wind. We will see the reasons for this in Chapter 5.

A line squall, typical of a cold front or trough of low pressure in cold air.

5 The life of a depression

Within the earth's atmosphere, depressions and anticyclones are continually developing and dying. Some last only a day or two; some, particularly the larger anticyclones, last for weeks on end. Some move quickly – they are the relatively shallow systems steered by the fast-flowing river of air in mid-latitudes. Some remain virtually stationary, particularly the larger anticyclones. There is an infinite variety. No two weather systems are ever identical. So in describing them we must be content with describing typical features and behaviour. It is a bit like observing a river of water from the bank. There is the main flow, normally (but not always) near the centre, while eddies in the flow are continually developing and then dying as they are carried away downstream. Most of the eddies form near the banks or where rocks interrupt the flow; just as in the earth's atmosphere most eddies form near the surface or in the lee of mountains.

The energy needed for the eddies in the river of water comes from the energy of the main flow as the water runs downhill. Energy to drive the eddies in the atmosphere comes both from the main flow and from local sources of heat, particularly latent heat. In temperate latitudes depressions are more likely to develop where warm and cold air masses meet, especially if there is plenty of moisture as well.

Typically, depressions affecting Western Europe develop over the Atlantic where cold polar air meets warm tropical air, and then move eastwards steered by the river of air aloft. This boundary between the warm and cold air is known as the *polar front* (figure 5.1). There is always much cloud near it since the relatively buoyant warm air likes to rise over the denser cold air. At the same time the cold air likes to push its nose under the warm air and lift it off the ground.

Birth

The first sign of a new depression is normally a wobble in the surface wind blowing near the polar front (figure 5.2).

Simultaneously the satellite picture will reveal thicker cloud, which speaks of latent heat being released and more energy becoming available for the cyclonic circulation to develop. As the new low develops a recognisable circulation it increasingly distorts the boundary between the cold and warm air masses (figures 5.3, 5.4), and within a matter of hours we have an advancing boundary of warm air – the warm front – ahead of the new low, and an advancing boundary of cold air behind it – the cold front – each with its typical cloud formation (see below).

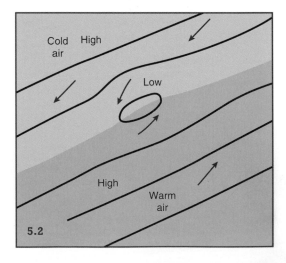

5.1

5.2

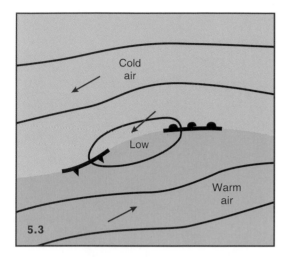

5.3

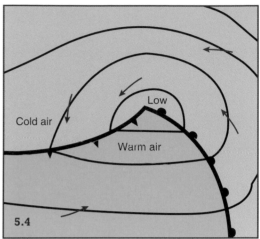

5.4

It must be emphasised that while it is useful to identify and describe typical cloud formations and sequences associated with warm and cold fronts, they are only typical. Just as no two depressions are ever identical so are no two fronts ever identical.

As the low develops the warm air will increasingly rise over the cold air ahead of it, and the cold air to the rear will increasingly undercut the warm air, in each case giving more cloud, more rain, and more energy to help drive the strengthening winds. The typical catalogue of events is as follows.

Days 1 and 2

The pressure falls, particularly along the fronts and in the region of the centre. Hence the pressure gradient increases and the wind strengthens (figures 5.4 and 5.5). The new low typically moves in the direction of the warm sector isobars, and may achieve speeds of 50 knots or more depending on the strength of the wind aloft. For the 3-dimensional picture turn to Appendix 2. It is useful to note that by simple geometry deep troughs will always have stronger pressure gradients and therefore stronger winds than shallow troughs of low pressure.

Days 2 and 3

As the low continues to deepen the distortion of the surface wind pattern extends steadily upwards, the low slows down, and typically turns to the left.

Since for a given pressure gradient cold air moves faster than warm air, the cold air behind the cold front gradually catches up with the warm front, pushing the warm air upwards and

out of the way, and we are left at the surface with an *occluded front* or *occlusion* (figure 5.6). The main troughs of the low continue to coincide with the fronts, but secondary troughs of low pressure may develop, particularly in the cold air on its left-hand side.These will be characterised by bands of thicker cloud and probably showers. Between the secondary troughs minor ridges may appear, characterised by mainly clear skies.

Days 3-6

After three to four days of growth and development the depression will be large and slow moving, with its centre usually somewhere between Iceland and Norway. Figure 5.7 is a typical example centred south of Iceland.

The fronts will become increasingly twisted around the centre and the cold front will trail away to the south-west or west, slotting into a trough which becomes shallower as you move away towards higher pressure. Typically the next stage is for a small wave depression to form on this cold front – which is still the polar front – usually between 300 and 500 miles from the centre of the parent low. It starts life just as the parent low did but frequently runs into the parent low and merges with it.

Sometimes the new wave depression will deepen even more than the parent low, and take up a position to the south or south-east of the original centre.

WARM FRONTS, COLD FRONTS AND OCCLUSIONS

Figures 5.8 and 5.9 describe typical cloud formations at cold and warm fronts. The surface

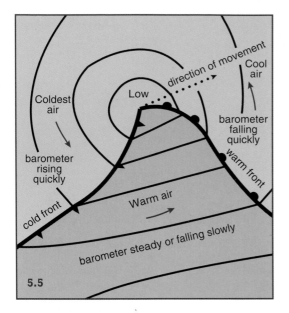

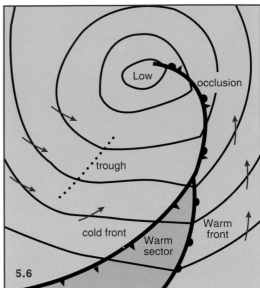

5.5

5.6

winds are shown by the arrows on the weather maps (figures 5.4, 5.5).

It is often possible also to observe the winds high up, especially in the advancing cirrus and alto-clouds ahead of the warm front (photograph opposite). These typically are fast moving and well veered on the surface wind, e.g. blowing from the north-west when the surface wind is southerly. The reason for this is explained in

Appendix 2. The stronger the upper level wind and the more veered it is, the more vigorous the advancing warm front. So this is a useful predictor of the weather a few hours ahead. With a cold front (figure 5.8) the higher clouds are often obscured until the front has passed, when you can look back (photograph opposite, below right) and see them moving from a direction that is well-backed from the surface wind – typically from the south or southwest when the surface

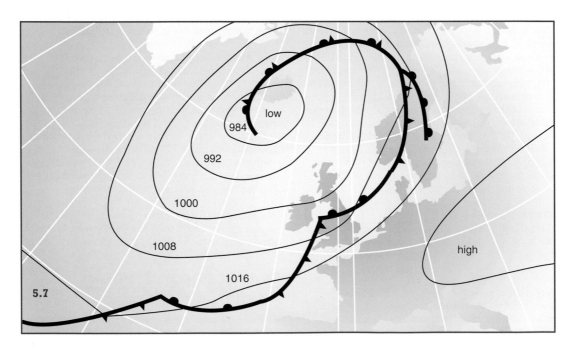

5.7

*Cirrostratus with typical halo ahead
of warm front.*

*Approach of a warm front (cirrus increasing
followed by altocumulus and altostratus.*

wind has veered to the west or north west. The
faster the higher clouds are moving the colder
and more showery the likely weather. Occluded
fronts have characteristics similar to warm or
cold fronts depending on whether the air ahead
is colder or warmer than the air behind (figures
5.10, 5.11).

WHERE DEPRESSIONS FORM

Some 60 per cent of depressions develop on the
polar front and evolve as I have just described.
An actual sequence with corresponding weather
maps and satellite pictures is shown on pages
30-31. This is only one example. Some move and
deepen very quickly, some slowly. Some have

sharply defined cloud patterns, some very
diffuse ones. Of the 40 per cent of depressions
which form other than on the polar front the most
common in western Europe are:

- In the lee of the mountains
- In cold air moving over warm sea
  – polar lows
- Over hot land areas in summer – heat lows.

An average weather map, for a month, will show
the most likely positions of low pressure and
high pressure, and is useful for planning a
voyage. But do not forget that it comprises a
great variety of day-to-day developments and
movements of weather systems.

*Warm sector (fractostratus with
altostratus above).*

*Looking north west as cold front moves
away south eastwards.*

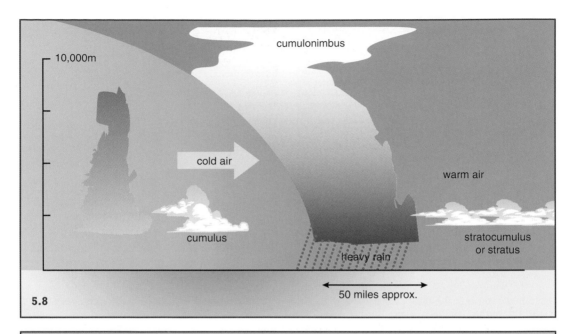

10,000m

cold air

warm air

cumulonimbus

cumulus

stratocumulus
or stratus

heavy rain

50 miles approx.

5.8

Typical sequence of weather associated with a warm front

	Front approaching	As it passes	In warm sector
Wind	increases & backs	veers	direction steady
Cloud	sequence of cirrus, cirrostratus, altostratus, nimbostratus, stratus	nimbostratus	stratus, stratocumulus
Rain	becomes heavier & more continuous	stops or turns to drizzle	occasional drizzle or light rain
Visibility	deteriorates slowly as rain gets heavier	deteriorates	moderate or poor; fog likely
Pressure	falls at increasing rate	stops falling	falls if depression deepening, otherwise steady
Dewpoint	little change	rises	little change

Typical sequence of weather associated with a cold front

	Front approaching	As it passes	In cold air behind it
Wind	backs & increases close to front	sudden veer often with squall	probably backs a little then direction steady; stronger & gusty
Cloud	stratus & stratocumulus thickening nimbostratus	cumulonimbus	often total clearance; cumulus develops
Rain	heavy rain near front	heavy rain, perhaps hail & thunder	usually fine for an hour or two, then showers
Visibility	moderate to poor, perhaps fog	poor in rain	very good
Pressure	falls near front	sudden rise	rise gradually levels off
Dewpoint	little change	sudden fall	little change

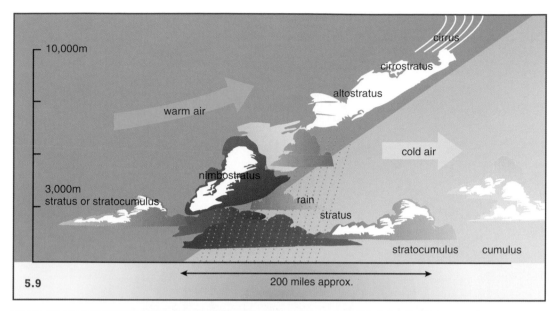

10,000m

warm air

cirrus

cirrostratus

altostratus

cold air

nimbostratus

3,000m
stratus or stratocumulus

rain

stratus

stratocumulus   cumulus

5.9

← 200 miles approx. →

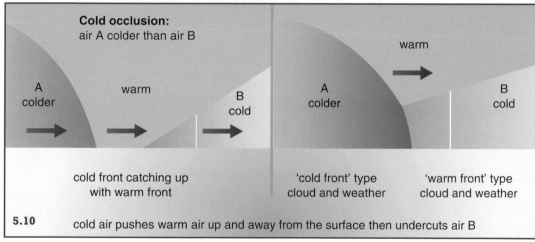

Cold occlusion:
air A colder than air B

A
colder

warm

B
cold

warm

A
colder

B
cold

cold front catching up
with warm front

'cold front' type
cloud and weather

'warm front' type
cloud and weather

5.10   cold air pushes warm air up and away from the surface then undercuts air B

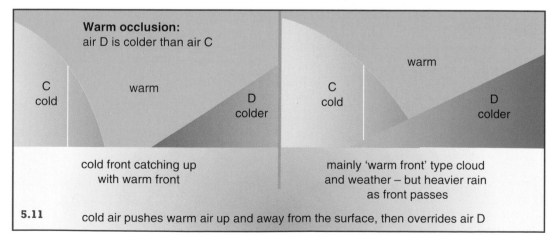

Warm occlusion:
air D is colder than air C

C
cold

warm

D
colder

C
cold

warm

D
colder

cold front catching up
with warm front

mainly 'warm front' type cloud
and weather – but heavier rain
as front passes

5.11   cold air pushes warm air up and away from the surface, then overrides air D

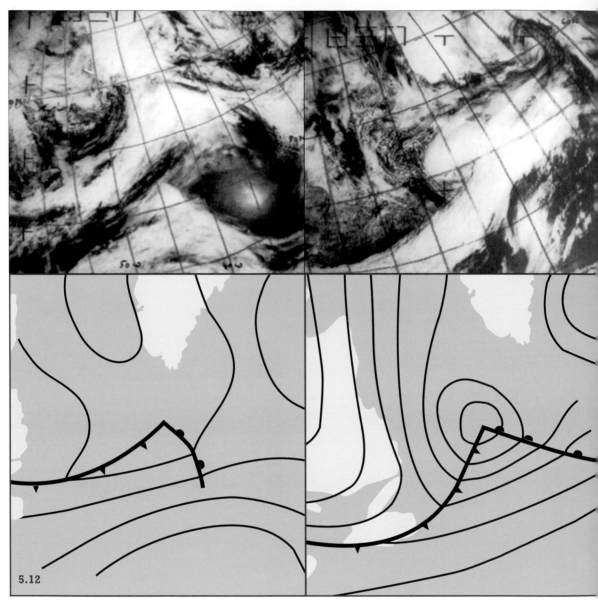

5.12

Day 1: newly formed depression,   Day 2: depression deepening rapidly.
often called a wave depression.

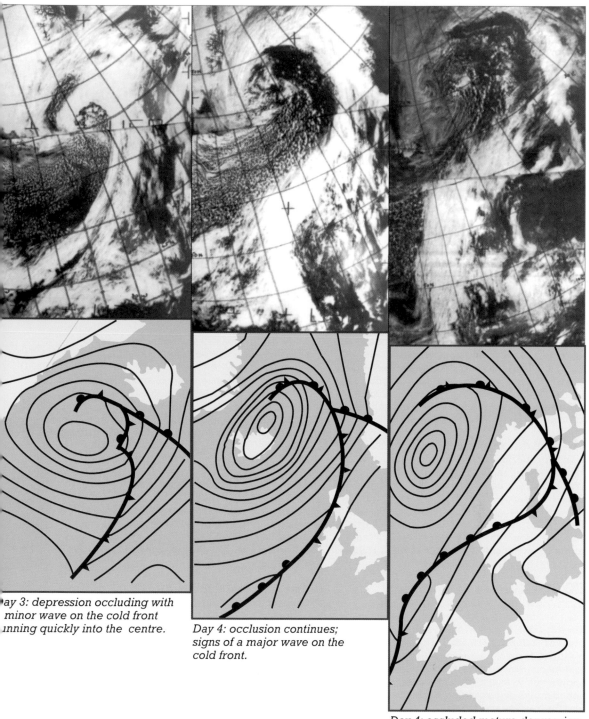

ay 3: depression occluding with
minor wave on the cold front
inning quickly into the centre.

Day 4: occlusion continues;
signs of a major wave on the
cold front.

Day 4: occluded mature depression.
Old centre decaying; major wave
developing on cold front.

6 Weather information
– sources and definitions

To forecast the weather with any accuracy more than a day or so ahead it is essential to take into account what is going on in every part of the world. Virtually every country in the world collects and exchanges weather information for the benefit of every other, and the language is international. Within 2 to 3 hours of the agreed data exchange times of 0000 and 1200 hours GMT, details of wind, temperature, pressure, etc from some 7000 land observing stations, over 500 ships at sea and about 500 upper air sounding stations are transmitted around the world, augmenting a continuous stream of data from weather satellites and providing essential 'ground truth'. Observations made regionally and nationally are exchanged at more frequent intervals. The amount of information exchanged is vast, and the whole operation is coordinated by the World Meteorological Organisation (WMO), probably the most efficient of all the specialised agencies of the United Nations.

Many national weather centres produce their own short period forecasts while relying on the world's major analysis and forecasting centres for predictions beyond a day or so. The Met Office at Bracknell and the European Centre at Reading are world leaders in forecasting and their products are used the world over. Say what you like about weather forecasts, you cannot improve on the output of the best meteorologists using the biggest computers.

SOURCES

Weather maps, text forecasts and observations are available from a wide variety of sources and in many different formats. Forecasts and weather information for the general public on radio and television provide useful background, but you should not go to sea without accessing more specific information including up-to-date actual and forecast weather maps. Most countries in Europe publish a menu of what is available for their coastal and sea areas. Details of times, frequencies and content of radio, telephone and facsimile services, and internet web sites can be found in RYA booklet G5 which is updated every year. Many telephone and facsimile services attract a premium charge rate.

NAVTEX AND GMDSS

Navtex provides for the automatic reception on board on a single international frequency – 518 kHz – of a printed sea area forecast twice daily and relevant gale warnings immediately they are issued. The text is always in English. Information provided also includes navigational and other warnings. The service is operational for many parts of the world including Europe and the Atlantic. Details of message indicators, times of broadcast, transmitting stations and areas covered will be found in RYA G5.

The Global Maritime Distress and Safety System (GMDSS), of which NAVTEX is an integral part, will provide for the worldwide automatic receipt on board of navigational and weather information in English transmitted by satellite (Inmarsat) via Standard-C. Details of broadcasts covering Europe and the north Atlantic are in G5.

WHAT THE WORDS MEAN

Fortunately most of the terminology used in weather bulletins, particularly those for sea areas, is internationally agreed and accepted. Translation into other languages will be found in RYA Booklet G5.

The General Synopsis
Most forecast bulletins start with a 'General Synopsis' giving the latest actual and predicted positions of the main features on the weather map. Many of the terms used – anticyclone, depression, front, etc are defined in Chapter 2. The following are some additional words related to the evolution of weather systems.

A **deepening** depression is one in which the central pressure is falling, and in which the winds and rain must be expected to increase. In a **filling** depression the reverse applies. A **vigorous** depression may be large or small and is characterised by strong winds and a lot of

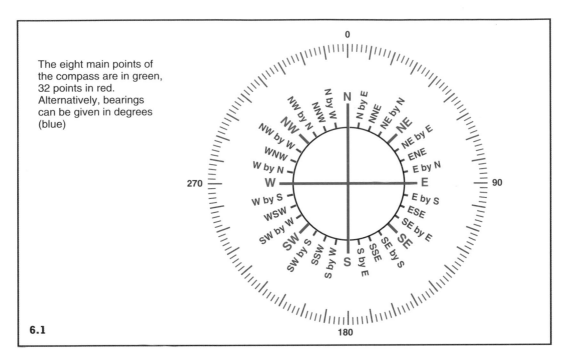

The eight main points of the compass are in green, 32 points in red. Alternatively, bearings can be given in degrees (blue)

6.1

rain. A **complex** depression has more than one centre of low pressure.

An anticyclone is said to **build** if its central pressure is rising, and to **decline** or **weaken** if its pressure is falling. If the pressure is falling quickly it is described as **collapsing**.

Troughs may fill or deepen independently of their parent depression, and sometimes a deepening trough will develop its own circulation. A new low so formed is called a **secondary depression**.

Speed of movement

The speed of movement of a depression or anticyclone is defined as follows:

Slowly	up to 15 knots
Steadily	15 to 25 knots
Rather quickly	25 to 35 knots
Rapidly	35 to 45 knots
Very rapidly	over 45 knots

Wind direction

This is given in either points of the compass or degrees, and is always the direction from which the wind is blowing. Figure 6.1 shows:
- an 8-point compass – normally used in forecasts
- a 32-point compass – often used in reporting observations
- a 360 degree compass.

Wind strength

In sea area forecasts wind strength is given in either Beaufort Force, knots or metres per second. Beaufort Force definitions are related to speed in knots in the table on page 34. One knot is one nautical mile per hour. To convert knots to metres per second, multiply by 0.52.

In land area forecasts descriptive terms are used, defined as follows:

Description	Beaufort force
calm	0
light	1-3
moderate	4
fresh	5
strong	6-7
gale	8

Gale warnings

Warnings are issued for:

Gales. If the mean wind is expected to increase to force 8 (34 knots) or over, or gusts of 43 knots or over are expected. Gusts as high as 43 knots may occur with the mean wind below 34 knots in unstable and showery airstreams.

Severe gales. If the mean wind is expected to increase to force 9 (41 knots) or over, or gusts of 52 knots or over are expected.

Storm. If the mean wind is expected to increase to force 10 (48 knots) or over, or gusts of 62 knots are expected.

Beaufort scale of wind force

Beaufort No.	General description	At sea	On land	Limits of velocity (knots)
0	Calm	Sea like a mirror	Calm; smoke rises vertically.	Less than 1
1	Light air	Ripples	Direction of wind shown by smoke drift but not by wind vanes.	1 to 3
2	Light breeze	Small wavelets	Wind felt on face; leaves rustle.	4 to 6
3	Gentle breeze	Large wavelets. Crests begin to break	Leaves and small twigs in constant motion. Wind extends light flags.	7 to 10
4	Moderate	Small waves becoming longer, fairly frequent white horses.	Raises dust and loose paper; small branches are moved.	11 to 16
5	Fresh breeze	Moderate waves, many white horses, chance of some spray.	Small trees in leaf begin to sway.	17 to 21
6	Strong breeze	Large waves begin to form; the white foam crests are more extensive everywhere. Probably some spray.	Large branches in motion. Umbrellas used with difficulty.	22 to 27
7	Near gale	Sea heaps up and white foam from breaking waves begins to be blown in streaks along the direction of the wind.	Whole trees in motion.	28 to 33
8	Gale	Moderately high waves of greater length; edges of crests begin to break into spindrift. The foam is blown in well-marked streaks along the direction of the wind.	Breaks twigs off trees; generally impedes progress.	34 to 40
9	Severe gale	High waves. Crests of waves begin to topple, tumble and roll over. Spray may affect visibility.	Slight structural damage (chimney pots and slates removed)	41 to 47
10	Storm	Very high waves with long overhanging crests. The resulting foam is blown in dense white streaks along the direction of the wind. On the whole the surface takes on a white appearance. The tumbling of the sea becomes very heavy and shock-like. Visibility affected.	Seldom experienced inland: trees uprooted; considerable structural damage occurs	48 to 55
11	Violent storm	Exceptionally high waves. The sea is completely covered with long white patches of foam lying along the direction of the wind. Everywhere the edges of the wave crests are blown into froth. Visibility affected.		56 to 63
12	Hurricane	Air filled with foam and spray. Sea completely white with driving spray. Visibility very seriously affected.		Greater than 63

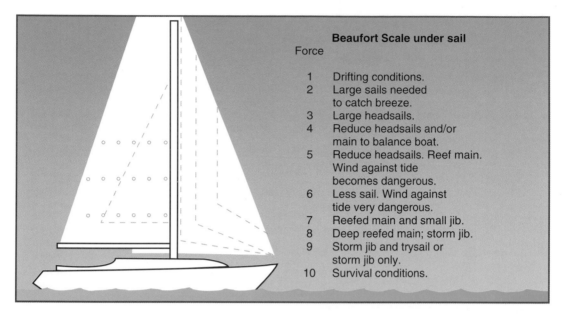

Beaufort Scale under sail

Force

1	Drifting conditions.
2	Large sails needed to catch breeze.
3	Large headsails.
4	Reduce headsails and/or main to balance boat.
5	Reduce headsails. Reef main. Wind against tide becomes dangerous.
6	Less sail. Wind against tide very dangerous.
7	Reefed main and small jib.
8	Deep reefed main; storm jib.
9	Storm jib and trysail or storm jib only.
10	Survival conditions.

The words 'imminent', 'soon', and 'later', have precise meanings as follows:
Imminent – within 6 hours of issue of the warning
Soon – 6-12 hours from time of issue
Later – beyond 12 hours from time of issue.

Visibility
In sea area forecasts visibility descriptions have the following meanings:

Description	Extent of visibilty
good	more than 5 nautical miles
moderate	2 to 5 nautical miles
poor	1000 metres to 2 nautical miles
fog	less than 1000 metres

In land area forecasts the fog limit is lower and the following terms are used:

Description	Extent of visibilty
fog	200 to 1000 metres
thick fog	less than 200 metres
dense fog	less than 50 metres

In coastal station reports and also in aviation forecasts the definitions are:

Description	Extent of visibilty
mist or haze	1000 to 2000 metres
fog	less than 1000 metres

Weather
This is not currently included in reports from automatic stations. In reports where it does appear the terms 'rain', 'snow', 'hail', etc., are obvious enough but the use of the word 'fair' needs defining. The weather is described as 'fair' when there is nothing 'significant' happening, i.e. no rain, fog, showers, etc. It may or may not be cloudy.

Pressure and pressure tendency
The general synopsis often gives the values of the pressure at the centres of the important weather systems, while the coastal station reports give recorded atmospheric pressure and also the pressure tendency. The international unit for measuring pressure is the millibar, sometimes known as the hectopascal. The terms used for pressure tendency in the coastal station reports are defined overleaf.

One must beware of reading too much into reports of 'rising slowly' and 'falling slowly', and also 'now falling' and 'now rising', if general pressure changes are small. Every day there are small ups and downs in pressure all over the world due to the atmospheric tide. In the south of Britain the tidal pressure variation is just under 1 mb. At the equator it is 3 mb. The highest values of pressure due to this tide occur at 1000 and 2200, the lowest at 0400 and 1600: the same local times everywhere in the world. So if at 0400 or 1600 the pressure is reported as 'falling slowly' it does not mean the weather is likely to or beginning to deteriorate. Similarly if at 1000 or 2200 the pressure is reported as 'rising slowly' it says nothing about improvement in the weather.

Description	Pressure tendency
steady	change less than 0.1 mb in 3 hours
rising slowly (falling slowly)	change 0.1 to 1.5 mb in last 3 hours
rising (falling)	change 1.6 to 3.5 mb in last 3 hours
rising quickly (falling quickly)	change 3.6 to 6.0 mb in last 3 hours
rising (falling) very rapidly	change of more than 6.0 mb in last 3 hours
now falling (now rising)	change from rising to falling (and vice versa) within last 3 hours

State of sea

Definition	Height of waves (metres)
calm – glassy	0
calm – rippled	0 to 0.1
smooth	0.1 to 0.5
slight	0.5 to 1.25
moderate	1.25 to 2.5
rough	2.5 to 4
very rough	4 to 6
high	6 to 9
very high	9 to 14
phenomenal	Over 14

FAX CHART INDICATORS

Many charts broadcast on radio facsimile are for aviation purposes and relate to winds and temperatures high up. Those you want are labelled 'surface' or identified by the letter 'S' in a coded heading. If the letters 'S' and 'U' appear together there will be two sets of lines, one for the surface and the other relating to the upper air. Other widely used identifiers are 'VT' for 'validity time', and 'PROG' for 'prognosis'. 'T+0' means the actual weather map for the time, 'T+24' a 24-hour forecast, 'T+48' a 48-hour forecast, and so on. Some charts, particularly those from Bracknell, provide a geostrophic wind scale in one corner. You will find instructions on how to use this scale on page 10. Some facsimile charts include plotted observations. These are always 'actual' charts for the time shown. If reception is good you may be able to read the details of the observations. The key to interpreting them is on pages 71 and 72.

7 DIY – Your own observations

You can receive weather charts, observations from buoys, ships and coast stations, and pictures from weather satellites, but there remains one all important piece in the construction of your weather jig-saw: your own observation – what the weather is doing where you are. This is unique to you. It is just as important as any other piece of information, and demands a place on your weather map.

Your observation is an integral part of the overall weather picture. If you are at sea it is particularly important, for whereas over land there is a good network of weather stations, at sea there are hardly any. Forecasters do their best to fill the gaps using information from weather satellites. These are a great help but they do not provide all the 'ground truth' for where you are. Your own observation is the key.

Enter your observations in your log at regular intervals, preferably at times which coincide with a weather chart, either a fax chart which will be for one of the 'main hours GMT' i.e. 0000, 0600,1200 or 1800; or the charts you construct yourself which will be for an 'intermediate' hour appropriate to the time of the coastal station reports included in the bulletin. If the weather is changing rapidly it will be worth making more frequent log entries.

You should observe and log the following:
1 Wind direction. An observation using hand–bearing compass and telltale will need correcting for boat movement.
2 Wind speed. An on-deck observation using a hand–held anenometer will need correcting for boat movement. If you have no instrument judge the wind speed in terms of Beaufort Force by looking at the sea surface and referring to the definitions on page 34. Remember that there will be a difference between masthead and deck readings of both wind speed and direction, depending on the height of your mast and the stability of the air. The deck reading will be the lighter and more backed.

3 Atmospheric pressure. It is the changes to pressure that matter most, but it does help to have your barometer or barograph reading correctly so that your observation fits the others on your weather map. Therefore it is worth checking your pressure reading with the nearest weather centre before you leave harbour and making any adjustments necessary.
Alternatively, when winds are light and the pressure almost uniform and observations from coast stations and light vessels near you are within a millibar of each other, set your barometer to this reading.

4 If you have a barograph, record whether the pressure is rising, falling or steady.
5 Visibility – in general terms (good, very good, poor).
6 Clouds. Keep your eye on the sky. Get used to looking at he clouds, the high ones as well as the low ones, and judging their speed of movement – not in absolute terms, but merely whether they are moving fast or slowly and from which direction. The clouds hold many clues to the weather in the next few hours.
7 State of sea. Note particularly the height, period (time between wave crests) and direction of any swell.
If you have a thermometer or hygrometer log their readings as well. The temperature of the sea water can be of interest too, especially if there is a risk of fog (Chapter 9) or you need more wind (Chapter 13). Part of a ship's weather log is shown overleaf (figure 7.1).

USING YOUR WEATHER OBSERVATION

Having made your observation, study it in relation to the latest available weather map – either the official version or one you constructed yourself. If the times are reasonably similar plot the observation on the map and see how it fits. Buys Ballot's Law (page 13) will help to get you orientated.

If the wind speed and direction are within 20 per cent and 20 degrees of the figures indicated by the isobars you can be reasonably confident that you have the overall picture of the weather. But if they do not fit, do not tear up the weather map

Cumulus spreading out into stratocumulus – typical of showers dying out and an approaching ridge.

or the forecast. Your observation cannot invalidate all the other information which went into the weather analysis and forecasting process.

Let us look at some possible reasons for a large discrepancy in wind speed and/or direction (a large discrepancy in pressure is much less likely).

1   If the wind is light – force 1 or 2 – it is not unusual to find an eddy, perhaps two or three miles across, moving downwind at about the same speed as the general wind given by the pressure pattern – a 'hole' in the wind. It might take up to an hour to cross you, and if your course and speed are the same as that of the eddy it could take much longer.

2   Is it a coastal effect? A sea or land breeze, for instance? These are not normally included in shipping bulletins, and they do not conform to the isobaric map. See Chapters 10 and 11.

3   Is it a detached remnant of the sea breeze? This is an interesting and far from unusual phenomenon. Following a good sea breeze day the sea breeze retreats from the shore as night falls and moves out seawards on the offshore gradient wind. Such an eddy may be from 2 to 10 miles across and will give a completely different wind for an hour or two. See Chapter 11.

4   Is it due to a thunderstorm or heavy shower? During its lifetime of 2–3 hours a storm is likely to generate its own winds. One wind will be taking air into the storm and another, usually preceded by a squall, will be taking cold air out of it.

If your observation disagrees with the forecast but fits the weather map, then it is worth checking that the forecast was for the area you are in. Did you write down the forecast or are you working from memory?

0900	Wind WSW force 3, pressure 1008 mb, half cover cloud, slight swell from SW, visibility good.	
1015	Light shower	
1200	Wind SW force 4, pressure 1007 mb, cloud increasing from west, swell from SW increasing, visibility good.	
1345	Rain started, wind backed to SSW and increased to force 5, barometer falling more rapidly, now 1005 mb.	
1500	Wind SSW force 5, raining quite heavily, pressure 1004 mb, steady swell from SW, visibility poor	
1520	Rain stopped, wind veered to WSW force 4, pressure now rising, clear sky to west, steady swell from SW, good visibility.	

7.1 *Part of a typical weather log.*

8 Weather maps and bulletins – how to use them

Interpreting a weather map is not an academic exercise remote from reality, any more than using a road map to show you where you have been, where you are, and where you want to go.

Whether you are about to set sail or are in mid-passage, thinking about the wind and weather follows the same logic:
- What has it been doing ? Keep a log of the wind, weather and pressure over the past few days, and relate your observations to the weather maps for the same period, so that you have on paper and in your mind a picture of how your wind and weather fits the overall pattern of recent movement and evolution of highs and lows.
- What is it doing? Your latest observation will probably be a few hours later than the latest available weather map, and to make it fit you will have to interpolate between the latest actual and forecast maps; all part of thinking simultaneously about how the weather map is changing and how your wind on the deck relates to the gradient wind.
- What is forecast? This means thinking through the sequence of wind, weather and barometer readings for the time you will be at sea, using the forecast maps along with written or voice forecasts.
- What coastal influences must you take into account? These are unlikely to be covered in a general forecast and you must work them out for yourself using the guidance in Chapters 10 and 11.
- What tidal influences must you take into account? Make sure you know the times of high and low water, the tidal streams for your area and what effect the wind will have on the waves (Chapter 13).

We now look in more detail at using and interpreting weather maps with some typical examples. But first a couple of general points:

- The wind is never absolutely constant or uniform over an area, so don't try to be too precise. Even over the open ocean and well away from the coast fluctuations of 10 to 15 degrees in direction and 10% to 20% in speed are not uncommon. See Chapter 12.
- Do not confuse the diurnal rise and fall in pressure of 1 to 2 millibars with small changes due to movement of weather systems (Chapter 1).

WEATHER MAP EXAMPLES

STRAIGHT ISOBARS – NO CHANGE FORECAST

Figure 8.1 is a typical weather situation with high pressure over northern Britain and an east to northeast wind in the English Channel where the isobars are fairly straight. The forecast is for no change, and you confirm this by checking your barometer readings. There is a small difference in gradient wind direction between sea areas Dover and Plymouth (see page 79), but over the whole area the direction on the deck would be described as northeasterly. But it is worth looking carefully at the wind speed indications. Measuring with your dividers the separation of the 1028 and 1024 millibar isobars gives a reading on the geostrophic scale (page 11) of between 12 and 16 knots, the stronger wind in the east, consistent with a wind on the deck in the range Force 3 to 4. However this reading is strictly valid only for the area mid-way between the two isobars, i.e. the northern side of the Channel. The 1024 and 1020 millibar isobars over northern France are much closer, giving a gradient wind there of some 30 knots, and indicating a stronger wind – Force 5 – on the south side of the Channel. You would come to the same conclusion if you pencilled in intermediate isobars for values 1026 and 1022 millibars – the requisite 4 millibar separation for use with the geostrophic scale.

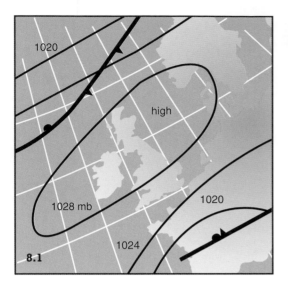

8.1

CURVED ISOBARS
– NO CHANGE FORECAST

The weather map in figure 8.2 shows a stationary anticyclone. The isobars over the Irish sea are fairly straight and the wind direction and speed can be derived in the same way as for figure 8.1. Over the North Sea and Channel however the lines are curved with large variations in direction from one side to the other in most sea areas. Shipping forecasts will summarise the wind as southeasterly for some of the Channel areas and southerly or southwesterly off the east coast of Britain, each covering a range of up to 45 degrees. However it is easily possible, looking at the weather map to get a much better idea of the wind direction and its variation, and you will often find this more precise information very useful. If you are sailing for instance from Hayling Island to Le Havre you might imagine that the forecast of a southeasterly wind would mean frequent tacks all the way, whereas with the wind backing through some 60 degrees during your passage you would benefit by spending much of the time on port.

MOVING WEATHER

With every weather situation
you have to think about:
• which way will the weather systems move
• how much will they change
The forecast will tell you in broad outline, but given a weather map, or preferably a sequence of weather maps, there is much useful detail you can work out yourself. Every weather situation is different, but the process of following through the changes is common to all. Here are three typical examples.

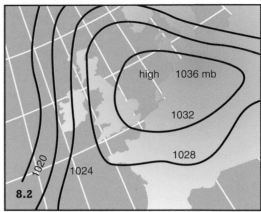

8.2

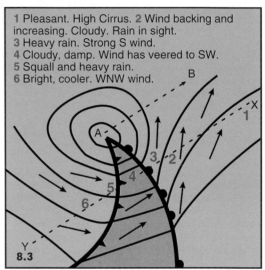

1 Pleasant. High Cirrus. 2 Wind backing and increasing. Cloudy. Rain in sight.
3 Heavy rain. Strong S wind.
4 Cloudy, damp. Wind has veered to SW.
5 Squall and heavy rain.
6 Bright, cooler. WNW wind.

8.3

A DEPRESSION MOVES EAST TO THE NORTH OF YOU

The depression in figure 8.3 is moving NE in the direction A-B, passing by within 12 hours or so. You are at X . The sequence of wind and weather changes at X as it goes by will be similar to that along line XY – not quite the same because the cold front will be moving faster than the warm front. The wind will:
• increase and back ahead of the warm front
• veer and decrease as the warm front passes and the air mass becomes more stable
• veer again as the cold front passes, with some increase in speed in the colder air

The sequence of pressure changes will follow the values given by the isobars along XY. The typical weather associated with the fronts is described in Chapter 5, and illustrated by the sequence of cloud photographs on page 27.

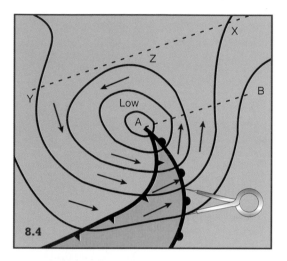

8.4

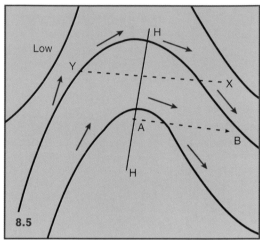

8.5

A DEPRESSION MOVES EAST TO THE SOUTH OF YOU

In figure 8.4, AB is the track of the depression, and XY the line depicting the wind changes you are likely to experience at X. There are no fronts crossing so sudden changes in wind speed and direction are unlikely. The wind at X will back from SW through east to become northerly. The pressure gradient becomes much slacker for a time and it is wise to assume that the wind at Z will be near the value given by the isobars to the south.

A RIDGE MOVES ACROSS YOU

You are at X and the ridge with axis H–H is moving east in the direction A–B (figure 8.5). The sequence of wind changes experienced at X will be similar to that along XY; northwesterly gradually backing and decreasing as the axis approaches and the pressure rises to a maximum – check with your barometer – then as the direction continues to back, a gradual increase in speed. No sudden changes are likely, unless the wind falls calm near the ridge axis when it often happens that the new wind, in this case southerly force 2 to 3, arises within a minute or two.

WEATHER SYSTEM DEEPENING OR FILLING

The above discussion of moving weather has assumed no change in the depth of the lows or the strength of the ridge. When the overall pressure is falling or rising the gradients will change accordingly and your estimates of the wind speeds will have to be revised upwards or downwards. Usually you will have an actual and forecast weather map available so that you can measure the wind speeds along your route on each map and interpolate between the two.

WHEN WILL THE FRONT GO THROUGH?

Fronts, warm, cold and occluded move at a speed proportional to the gradient at right angles to them – 90% of gradient in the case of cold fronts and cold occlusions; in the region of 75% of gradient in the case of warm fronts and warm occlusions. So set your dividers to the distance between two isobars *along the line of the front*, measure the speed on the appropriate geostrophic scale and correct it for the type of front (figure 8.4)

TROUBLESHOOTING

- You are beating into a southwesterly in the Irish Sea. The wind is up to the limit of what was forecast, it is cloudy and raining and you are getting cold feet! Is the forecast going wrong? Check your barometer. Is it reading what you would expect from the weather maps? Yes! Then don't worry. If however it is beginning to fall more rapidly below the forecast values prepare for a stronger blow.

- You are making a night passage across the Channel. You left Cherbourg at dusk with a forecast for Wight and Portland of northwest 3 to 4. For the past few hours you have made 5 knots to the northeast, but now at 0300 the wind has dropped out. Wrong forecast? Two questions to ask are 'Is your barometer reading still consistent with the weather map?,' 'Did the midnight forecast still predict a nortwesterly 3 to 4?' If the answer to both is 'yes' then don't worry, you are almost certainly experiencing the dying remains of yesterday's sea breeze on the English coast (Chapter 11) and within a couple of hours your northwesterly will return.

9 Weather hazards

What is that black cloud to windward – does it indicate a squall, a gale, a thunderstorm, fog, or is it just a patch of dirty, smoke-laden air? There are a number of questions you can ask which will at least help toward an answer, and may rule out some hazards, as follows:

- What was the latest weather forecast?
- What is the barometer doing?
- Has the wind changed in the last hour or two (speed and direction)?
- Have the waves changed? Is there any swell?
- What have the higher clouds been doing? Have they been typical of those ahead of a front or trough? Did you notice which way they were moving?
- Are you within ten miles of land?

All this information you should have in your log. It is important to refer to the facts, not your crew's ideas or hunches as to what may have happened recently.

GALES

Gales which are due to depressions (squalls are very short-lived in comparison and are considered separately) do not spring up without warning, and with information in your log which will enable you to answer the above questions you will never be caught unawares. Watch out in particular for:

1 The weather forecast. If the possibility of a gale has been mentioned keep a listening watch on Radio 4 or the nearest coast radio station.

2 Your barometer. A fall of pressure of over 8 mb in three hours is almost certain to be followed by a gale whatever the wind is to start with, and a fall of over 5 mb in three hours by a force 6. If the wind is already force 7 you must expect a gale within an hour, but if it is only force 3 when your barometer starts falling at this rate you have at least three to four hours before the gale arrives. A very rapid rise in pressure after a trough has passed is also indicative of a gale, and the same rates of pressure change apply – a rise of over 6 mb in three hours for a force 8 and over 5 mb in three hours for a force 6. (You

must make allowances for your own movement, either towards or away from the low pressure – Buys Ballot's law will tell you which way you are going relative to the pressure centre.)

These rapid pressure changes are certain signs of a gale. They were in the 1979 Fastnet Race, when virtually all other signs were missing. But don't assume that because the barometer is not falling rapidly a gale is impossible. It will take longer to arrive, but all the other signs are important as well.

3 If the wind is both backing and increasing it indicates a trough approaching, and you should find that the barometer is falling as well. If the black cloud of the trough is almost upon you the signs are of a temp-orary squall rather than a prolonged gale.

4 Waves on the sea produced by the local wind tell you no more than the wind itself, but swell waves can be a useful predictor. If they are increasing from the direction in which you know there is a depression an increase in wind is likely. Since swell waves take a long time to generate they usually indicate the approach of a large area of stronger winds which are likely to last for days rather than hours. There were no warning swell waves ahead of the 1979 Fastnet storm because the storm only developed as the first boats were approaching the Fastnet Rock.

5 High clouds increasing from the direction of lower pressure and travelling from a direction well veered on the surface wind (eg southerly surface wind and northwesterly upper wind) are a sign of increasing wind. The faster the high clouds are travelling the greater the likely increase in surface wind during the next six to twelve hours (see Appendix 2).

6 If the wind is blowing approximately along the coast so that with your back to the wind the coast is on your right–hand side, a force 6 to 7 wind either in harbour or 8 or more miles off the coast means a gale force 8 in a band within about 5 or 6 miles of the coast (see Chapter 11).

Altocumulus castellanus – heralding thundery weather.

SQUALLS

Two different types of squall are met in practice, one due to thunderstorms which we deal with below, and one associated with either a cold front or a trough of low pressure in relatively cold air. Typically some miles ahead of such a trough you may be able to see a line of towering cumulus clouds, and along the line of the trough itself the clouds are dense and black with patches of heavy rain. Absence of swell waves, only a slow fall in pressure and no preceding increase in high cloud moving from a well veered direction all suggest a very temporary squall lasting not more than about half an hour, if that. The best advice is to reef and make for the lightest part of the cloud. Having weathered the squall you can usually assume that another one is unlikely for three to four hours.

THUNDERSTORMS

The dark mass of threatening cloud associated with a mature thunderstorm is often heralded by a decrease in wind and an almost glassy sea. These features clearly distinguish it from a depression or trough. The barometer may move up and down quite quickly and erratically by one or two millibars, but again the absence of a longer period fall distinguishes this from an approaching depression. The best rule to avoid the worst of the wind is to leave the storm to port. Squalls associated with the storm usually move steadily outwards from the centre with the wind ahead of them in the opposite direction, that is blowing in towards the storm.

Near the coast thunderstorms are more likely in the afternoon and early evening when land temperatures are at a maximum. Over the open ocean thunderstorm frequency is highest at night when cloud–top temperatures are their lowest. As we saw in Chapter 1, this creates conditions of minimum stability over the sea.

For safety from lightning remember that tall, free–standing objects tend to be focal points for the electrical discharge to earth. So make sure that the conducting route (metal) through to the water is continuous. The crew are safe sitting well away from the mast and shrouds.

FOG

Two main types of fog are met at sea; fog which has formed over land on a cool, clear night and drifted out over the water; and sea fog which forms over the sea itself when relatively warm moist air moves over colder water.

Cumulonimbus and shower.

Drifting patches of land fog tend to lift to 3 to 6 metres or so above the sea surface and gradually break up as they move away from the coast. The warmer the water compared to the temperature of the air over the land, the quicker the fog disperses. So if you are in fog in harbour and the forecast is for fog over land clearing during the morning, you can safely sail out to sea expecting the fog to be gone by the time you return to port.

Sea Fog

Sea fog forms typically in tropical maritime air as it moves northwards over colder waters. Expect it for instance in warm, moist southwesterly winds blowing in from the Azores or further south. The critical factors are the dewpoint of the air and the temperature of the sea surface.

The dewpoint of any particular mass of air is defined as the temperature to which it must be cooled for condensation to occur, that is for fog to form. Air from warm sea areas to the southwest arrives with a high dewpoint, often higher than the sea surface temperature around Britain, so it becomes characteristically foggy. Air originating over dry land or cold seas has a low dewpoint, usually well below the sea surface temperature around Britain and is not associated with fog.

Hill fog and sea fog (stratus) – with stratocumulus and altostratus above.

When the dewpoint value is marginal the incidence of fog relates to the variation in sea temperature. In winter and spring the sea is coldest inshore so fog forms more frequently inshore than out to sea. In summer and autumn the sea is coldest away from the shore so fog forms more frequently out to sea. There are always variations in sea temperature from place to place and consequently variations in sea fog. Many changes in sea temperature are due to the tide, so the position and extent of fog banks alter with changes in the tide.

If the dewpoint of the air is everywhere well above the sea temperature, widespread or

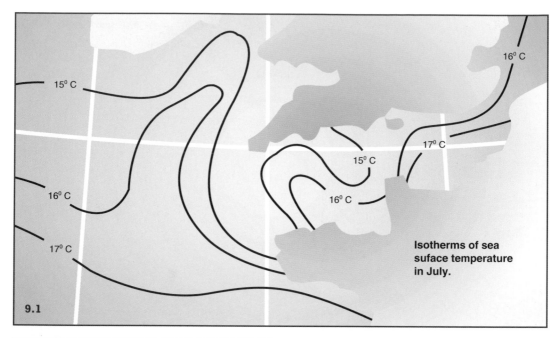

15⁰ C

16⁰ C

15⁰ C

17⁰ C

16⁰ C

16⁰ C

17⁰ C

Isotherms of sea suface temperature in July.

9.1

Satellite picture showing an area of sea fog moving around the north of Scotland.

The sample of sea surface temperature isotherms for a typical five–day period in July (figure 9.1) illustrates how variable the temperature is. If the dewpoint of air moving in on southwesterly winds was 15 degrees C, fog would be widespread south of Cornwall and in the Bristol Channel, but the coastal waters off northern France would be largely clear.

As a sea fog gets older its characteristics gradually change: it becomes colder and heavier, and immune to variations in sea temperature. The 'haar' which sometimes envelops the coasts of north and east Scotland is of this type. It starts life in warm, moist southerly winds moving over colder seas around Ireland. By the time it reaches Scotland a day or more later it has cooled many degrees (by radiation from the top of the fog) and become a very wet and persistent fog with few if any breaks except in the lee of the land.

STEEP WAVES

A change in wind direction, or a change in tide may mean a change to a wind–against–tide situation. Beware! This can lead very quickly to a dangerously steep sea. The reason is as follows.

The height of waves depends on:

- the strength of the wind
- for how long and over what distance it has been blowing

extensive fog is forecast. If it is only a little above sea temperature, and in some cases may not be so, fog banks are forecast. If the dewpoint of the air is above the sea temperature only in a few places fog patches are forecast, and coastal fog in winter and spring.

If you are caught in widespread fog there is little you can do other than sail to the lee of the nearest land or wait for the next cold front.

"According to the wind indicator it's easing off."

When there is a current running the wave height remains at the value appropriate to the wind strength, but the distance apart (wavelength) changes. It is reduced when the current is running against the wind, and increased when it is with the wind. A shorter wavelength means a steeper wave. Currents:

• off headlands such as Portland Bill
• over ledges such as the Needles
• through races such as the Little Russel
• through narrows such as Corryvrechan

can be strong enough to reduce the wavelength by over 50% in an opposing wind, giving very steep and dangerous seas. Conversely the increase in wavelength when tide and wind are running in the same direction will make life a lot easier.

Cartoon reproduced from one of Mike Peyton's cartoon books, also published by Fernhurst Books.

10 Winds near coasts

We now look at bends and bands in the wind which are found near coasts and downwind of hills and islands; not mere puffs in the wind but substantial changes in direction and speed, large enough to influence a decision to go or not to go. In fact, whenever the wind is blowing offshore or along the shore its speed and direction are influenced by the presence and shape of the coast. The bends and bands rarely feature in a forecast, you have to sort them out for yourself – and you can, given the guidance which follows. Sea breezes, another important feature of coastal winds, will be discussed separately in Chapter 11.

Wind blowing off the shore

If the wind is blowing from the land, whatever the angle of the wind to the coastline, the direction will always veer and the speed increase as the wind moves out over the water (figure 10.1). Some books state incorrectly that the effect is refraction, and that the wind changes direction towards a line at right angles to the land. This is not so. We have already seen – Chapter 3 – that for a given pressure gradient the wind over the land is 20 to 30 degrees back from the wind over the nearby water. So whatever the angle of the wind to the shoreline, its direction veers as it moves out over the water. This means that it often pays to make for harbour on port tack. You must expect to be headed if you approach land close-hauled on starboard.

Wind blowing along the shore

There is a major difference when the wind is blowing along the coast, depending on whether the land is to your left or your right hand when standing with your back to the wind.

If the coast is to your right the surface winds over land and water are convergent for the same pressure gradient wind (figure 10.2). This results in a band of stronger wind within two to three miles of the shore. The increase in speed in the band is normally of the order of 25 per cent, e.g about 5 knots added to a 20 knot wind. Also because of the convergence of the airstreams the air is forced upwards, often giving an increase in cloud or a bank of thicker cloud along the coast.

The stronger wind just offshore is often mistaken for a sea breeze but in fact it persists day and night. So if you put out from harbour on the south coast of England in an easterly wind and find it force 5 instead of the expected force 4 you can be reasonably sure that by the time you are three or four miles off the coast it will have dropped to the lower speed you were hoping for. Equally, when you are approaching a coast where the land and sea winds are converging be prepared for an increase in the red zone of figure 10.2.

When, standing with your back to the wind, the coast is on you left-hand side, the effect is the opposite (figure 10.3). The airstreams diverge, the wind is that much lighter near the shore and there is less cloud than elsewhere because the air is being drawn downwards. This is why the sunniest seaside resorts are often found where the prevailing wind is westerly on a south-facing coast, easterly on a north-facing coast, and so on. Note however that in the afternoons this lack of wind near the coast is often overridden by a sea breeze (see Chapter 11).

Wind blowing onto the shore

There is no significant variation in the wind over the water. All of the changes occur over land

Coastal cliffs

When the wind is blowing along the shore and the land and sea winds are converging the presence of cliffs may add another knot or two to the wind close to the coast.

When the wind is blowing off the shore, standing waves often form in the wind downwind from the

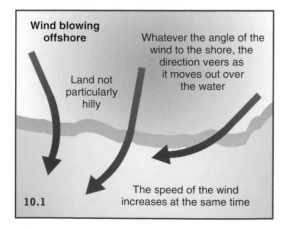

Wind blowing offshore

Land not particularly hilly

Whatever the angle of the wind to the shore, the direction veers as it moves out over the water

The speed of the wind increases at the same time

10.1

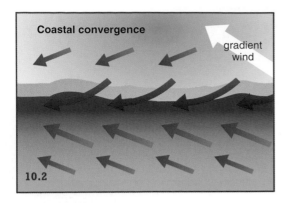

Coastal convergence
gradient wind

10.2

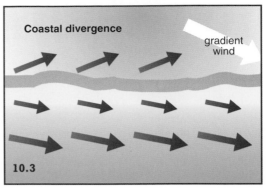

Coastal divergence
gradient wind

10.3

cliff face (figure 10.4) and give relatively static zones of stronger and lighter wind, sometimes marked by a cloud sitting on top of the lighter wind zones. The zones of stronger wind are the more reliable and are likely to remain in nearly the same place for as long as the wind direction and stability of the airstream do not change. The zones of lighter wind may be characterised by considerable variations, even reversals in wind direction, particularly downwind of the higher cliffs, but the positions of the zones themselves are likely to stay put for some time. Beneath the cliff itself there is usually a large eddy in the flow of air with a reversal in wind direction.

An island

A mountainous island clearly obstructs the wind, and nor surprisingly its influence extends many miles downwind. The Canaries are a good example. Here large eddies form in the air flow, often some fifty to a hundred miles across, and move away downwind, dispersing only slowly. Satellite pictures quite often reveal a string of three or four eddies, the furthest being some two or three hundred miles away from the islands.

Even a small, flat island has a significant influence on the wind. The air flowing over it slows down and its direction backs some 15 degrees. Along one side of the island there is a zone of stronger wind due to converging air-streams, and along the other side a zone of lighter wind due to diverging airstreams (figure 10.5).

These zones of stronger and lighter wind are not limited to the island shore but continue downwind for many miles. Sometimes a line of cloud provides evidence of the stronger wind band, and a line of blue sky or thinner cloud evidence of the lighter wind band.

Land breezes

These are found near coasts at night or in the early morning, usually when the sky is clear.

They are not the opposite of sea breezes. The best way to visualise them is as 'drainage' winds. Air that has cooled over the land on a clear night, being relatively dense, drains downwards, usually following valleys, until it reaches the sea. Its momentum carries it a mile or two out to sea before it warms up and dies away.

The direction of a land breeze is controlled almost entirely by the contours of the land. The cold air flows down the valleys and on reaching the sea spreads out fanwise. The steeper the slope, the stronger the breeze.

Mountain and valley winds

In mountainous areas some form of drainage wind is frequently experienced, either as a result of cold air accumulating in valleys until it breaks away like a bursting dam, or because cold air from behind a cold front piles up against a mountain barrier until it finds a way out. Both types of wind can arise suddenly, and both exhibit some diurnal variation. They tend to be strongest in the early morning and lightest in the afternoon.

MEDITERRANEAN WINDS

The most notable winds that affect the Mediterranean are essentially mountain and valley winds. The mountain ranges, from the Pyrenees in the west through the Alps to the Taurus Mountains in the east, are high enough to block the southward movement of cold fronts. The cold air piles up against the mountains, and a day or two after the arrival of the front it starts escaping down the main valleys or through mountain gaps. The Rhone valley is one route south and the local wind is called the *Mistral*. Normally there is enough cold air available to keep the *Mistral* going for several days, and it often contributes to the formation of a depression in the Ligurian Sea. Typically the wind strength is Force 6 to 8, sometimes severe gale Force 9.

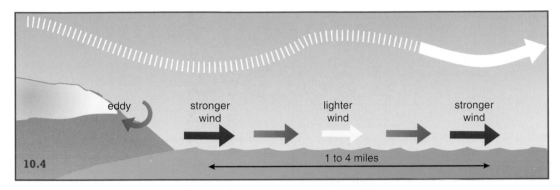

10.4

eddy | stronger wind | lighter wind | stronger wind

1 to 4 miles

Further east we have the *Bora* and *Tramontana* carrying cold air into the Adriatic Sea, and the *Gregale* and *Verdarro* which carry cold air into the Ionian and Aegean Seas. The *Etesian* or *Meltemi* is more feared in the Aegean: it has some of the characteristics of cold air spilling south but is essentially the funnelling of a gradient northeasterly wind from the Black Sea. It may persist for several days at a time, blowing at Force 6 to 7.

The south coast of Turkey experiences a more gentle northerly gradient in summer, encouraging moderate sea breezes by day and land breezes by night, making the area ideal for leisure sailing.

Two gap winds of the western Mediterranean are the *Vendeval* and *Levanter*. The *Vendeval* is a strong westerly emerging from the Straits of Gibraltar, and the *Levanter* a strong easterly being squeezed between Spain and Morocco as it approaches the same Straits.

The *Ghibli, Scirocco* and *Khamsin* are all southerlies which blow off the North African

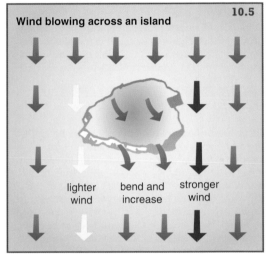

10.5

Wind blowing across an island

lighter wind | bend and increase | stronger wind

deserts; they are typically hot and dry. The *Leveche* and *Chili* are also hot winds from North Africa, but their warmth is as much due to their descent down the north slopes of the Atlas Mountains as to their desert origin. Such winds are normally known as *föhn* winds.

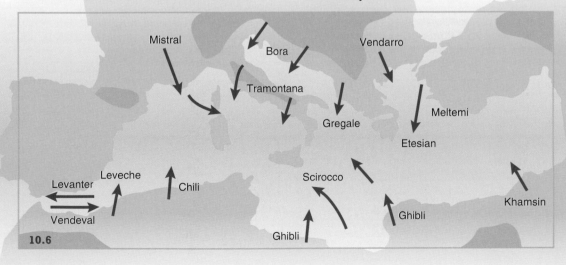

10.6

11 Afternoon winds and sea breezes

Whenever the day is bright or sunny the rise in temperature of the land affects the wind on the coast. The change is often small, only 3 or 4 knots, up or down; but sometimes the wind near the coast increases by as much as 20 knots, enough to have serious consequences for your comfort and safety. Fortunately it is not difficult to predict these changes yourself in the afternoon wind. Everything depends on the direction of the gradient wind in relation to the shoreline.

GRADIENT WIND BLOWING ONSHORE

For a gradient wind blowing onshore the change in wind from morning to afternoon due to heating of the land is summarised in figure 11.1. If the wind speed is already at your limit for safety and comfort don't set sail when the direction is in the pink zone; it will get stronger. Equally if the direction is in the yellow zone and you have only 4 or 5 knots at midday expect near calm conditions in the afternoon and do not rely on wind to help you stem the tide.
The reason is simply that heating of the land causes the pressure over the land to fall by 3 or 4 millibars. If the pressure is lower over the land than over the water to start with, as it is for wind directions in the pink zone, the extra fall in pressure due to heating causes a small increase in wind. If the pressure starts higher over land than over the water heating reduces the gradient and the wind drops. Buys Ballot's Law will help you relate the wind direction to whether the pressure is relatively high or low over the land. You may have noted that afternoon heating tends

temporarily to reduce the effects of coastal convergence and divergence which we discussed in Chapter 10.

THE SEA BREEZE

The term 'sea breeze' is often used very loosely for any wind blowing onshore. But it is important, particularly for safety reasons to distinguish between:
* onshore winds which are due to an onshore gradient wind, whose characteristics we have just discussed; and
* genuine sea breezes which arise with an offshore gradient wind and may reach 20 knots or more (subject to the gradient wind being less than 20 knots).

Figure 11.2 summarises the essential initial stages of the genuine sea breeze. A typical development sequence on a straight stretch of coast facing any direction is as follows:
* Day starts sunny or bright with only thin cloud; land temperature rises above sea temperature; air warmed over land expands creating an imbalance aloft.
* Air aloft is carried seawards, helped by the offshore gradient wind, where it subsides, dispersing any cloud just offshore.
* Subsiding air feeds a gentle drift on to the shore, killing and undercutting the offshore wind and completing the circulation.
* Sea breeze extends steadily inland, and subsiding zone extends steadily seawards preceded by a calm zone.
* More and more air is drawn into the shore

wind increases by 4-6 knots

Small change in wind speed (less than 4 knots)

wind drops by 4-6 knots

11.1

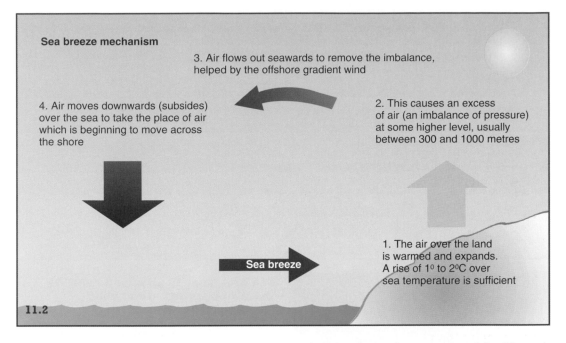

Sea breeze mechanism

3. Air flows out seawards to remove the imbalance, helped by the offshore gradient wind

4. Air moves downwards (subsides) over the sea to take the place of air which is beginning to move across the shore

2. This causes an excess of air (an imbalance of pressure) at some higher level, usually between 300 and 1000 metres

Sea breeze

1. The air over the land is warmed and expands. A rise of 1⁰ to 2⁰C over sea temperature is sufficient

11.2

and the breeze builds. It is always strongest near the shore (figure 11.3).

- Sea breeze direction swings to the right (looking upwind) (figure 11.4). This is because of Coriolis Force.
- By mid-afternoon sea breeze reaches about 30 miles inland and 20 miles or more seawards.
- Direction steadies at about 20 degrees from the shoreline. Strength near coast Force 4 to 6, decreasing seawards (figure 11.4).
- Sea breeze dies away as sun sets. Dying remains of sea breeze circulation move away offshore on the gradient wind and may be found 40 miles or more away downwind before disappearing (figure 11.5).

The same thinking can be applied to the development of a sea breeze on to any other shape of coast, except that you also have to ask:

- is there plenty of room to move inland ?
- is there a plentiful supply of air from over the sea ?

Two examples of the development of a sea breeze in the absence of a gradient wind will show the sort of limitations which may arise.

Sea breeze onto an island – no gradient wind

The supply of air from over the water is clearly unlimited. But if the island is small, the sea breeze which starts blowing on to all the shores (figure 11.6) will soon have nowhere to go and cool air from the sea will cover the whole island. The calm will then return, but as the air over the island warms again a new breeze will develop and the same sequence will be repeated. The interval between repeats depends on the size of the island. For one about 5 miles across it will be less than an hour.

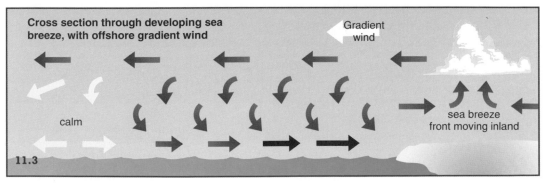

Cross section through developing sea breeze, with offshore gradient wind

Gradient wind

calm

sea breeze front moving inland

11.3

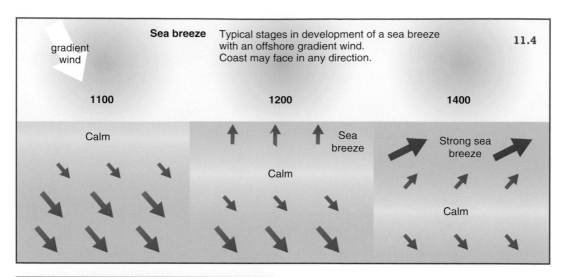

Sea breeze on to an island near the mainland – no gradient wind

If the island is the size of the Isle of Wight it cannot sustain a sea breeze for long. But neither can the channel between the island and the mainland. The initial sea breezes on to both the island and the mainland will soon exhaust the available air and a calm will return (figure 11.7). The process of develop and die will then be repeated. In the Solent the initial efforts at a sea breeze last for about 20 minutes. Eventually, however, the mainland sea breeze takes over and largely swamps the others.

Sea breeze on to any shape of coast – gradient wind blowing

If a gradient wind is blowing the sea breeze will develop only on to the coasts where the direction of the gradient wind is offshore and its development will depend on how much land there is upwind or how much sea downwind. An onshore gradient wind prevents the development of a genuine sea breeze because it opposes the offshore flow aloft necessary to feed the breeze

Cumulus along the coast marking the edge of the sea breeze front as it starts to move inland.

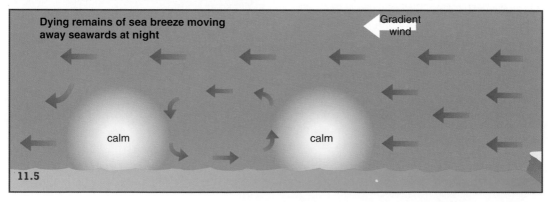

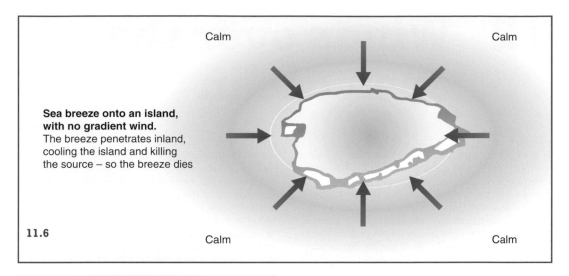

Sea breeze onto an island, with no gradient wind.
The breeze penetrates inland, cooling the island and killing the source – so the breeze dies

Calm

Calm

Calm

Calm

11.6

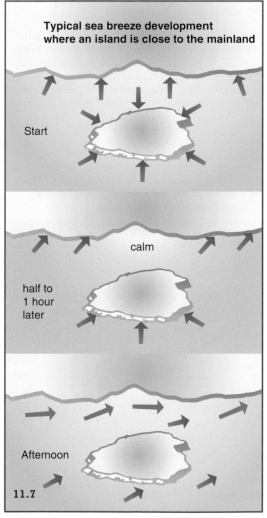

Typical sea breeze development where an island is close to the mainland

Start

calm

half to 1 hour later

Afternoon

11.7

lower down (figure 11.2). A much fuller discussion of sea breezes is provided in 'Wind Strategy', also published by Fernhurst Books.

SUMMARY

Figure 11.1 summarises how the afternoon coastal winds change when the gradient wind is blowing onshore

Figure 11.8 summarises how the afternoon coastal winds change when the gradient wind is blowing offshore and is less than 20 knots. You should beware of the red zone, especially when the tide is running against the wind.

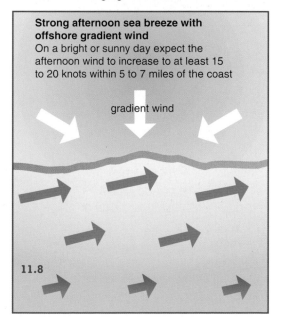

Strong afternoon sea breeze with offshore gradient wind
On a bright or sunny day expect the afternoon wind to increase to at least 15 to 20 knots within 5 to 7 miles of the coast

gradient wind

11.8

12 Winds over the open ocean

It is a misconception to think of the wind as being uniform for a given pressure gradient. It is not, even over a perfectly smooth sea – if such a thing were possible. The wind likes blowing in bands. The most striking example of this is the trade winds which are characterised by lines of 'trade wind cumulus' extending over hundreds of miles. These lines of cloud are evidence of what are called 'vortex rolls' where superimposed on the horizontal motion of the air is a vertical circulation of air moving slowly up into the lines of cloud and down into the clear lanes between (figure 12.1). These cloud lanes are typically 1 to 3 miles apart and the wind somewhat stronger and more veered in the clear lanes than under the clouds.

Even in the absence of cloud, or beneath a uniformly grey and cloudy sky, wind bands will be found over the open sea. The difference in strength between adjacent light and strong bands may be anything from 10 to 25 per cent, and their distance apart from 1 to 5 miles. Near the coast the position of the bands will normally be fixed by some feature of the coast or by the coastline itself, particularly when the wind is nearly parallel to it. Well away from the coast, the bands will move slowly due to the component of the pressure gradient wind across them (figure 12.2). Thus if you are sailing on the open sea, at least 5 miles from land, and the wind is lighter than it should be, it is advisable to sail on port tack (or gybe) until you find the stronger wind. Having found it, change to starboard tack to enable you to stay in the stronger wind as long as possible.

If the gradient wind is less than about 10 knots the bands tend to deform, and sometimes large (5 to 10 miles across) eddies appear in the wind. These 'holes' move down the gradient wind, so if you get into one the best way to get out is to make way towards the gradient wind direction.

CHANGES IN WATER TEMPERATURE

A sudden change in water temperature of a few degrees is almost as significant as a coastline in influencing the wind. Over colder water the

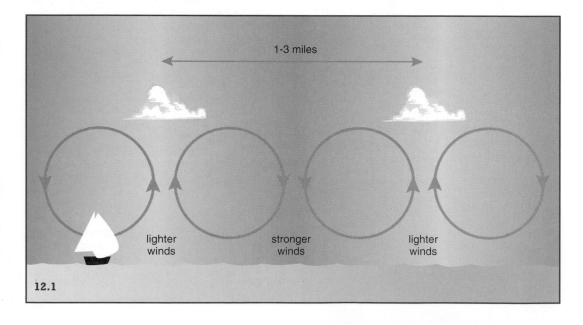

1-3 miles

lighter winds   stronger winds   lighter winds

12.1

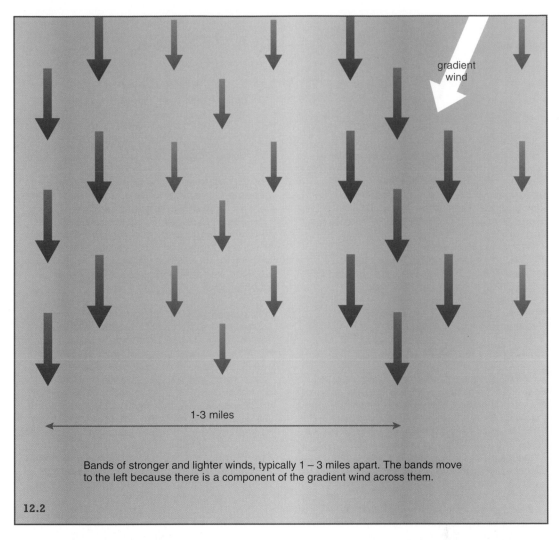

1-3 miles

Bands of stronger and lighter winds, typically 1 – 3 miles apart. The bands move to the left because there is a component of the gradient wind across them.

12.2

surface air will be cooled and become more stable, there will therefore be less vertical mixing and friction will cause the wind to back and slow down. Over warmer water the surface air will be warmed and become less stable, there will be more vertical mixing and the effect of friction will be more readily overcome, so the wind will be stronger and more veered.

The zone or dividing line between cold and warm water will act as a 'coastline'. There will be a bend as the air moves from one to the other, the bend always on the side downwind of the transition. For winds blowing along the transition a zone of convergence and stronger winds – or divergence and lighter winds – will be found, depending upon the direction; also the wind will be generally stronger over the warmer water than over the cold.

It is not uncommon to find water temperature changes of 4 to 5 degrees C, particularly near estuaries or where there are large areas of tidal upwelling.

If the stability of the air is critical (ie the air is stable to the temperature over one area of water and unstable to the temperature of the adjacent area) the differences in wind speed between the two areas could be as high as 25 per cent, but the areas must be several miles across to be fully effective.

Across the Gulf Stream you find dramatic changes in wind speed in only a few miles as the water temperature changes – typically from 10 knots over the cold water to 20 to 25 knots over the adjacent warm water.

13 Waves, swell, wind and tide

There are two different types of waves: wind waves, which are produced locally by the wind blowing at the time, and swell waves, which are generated by the wind somewhere else. The 'somewhere else' can be thousands of miles away. The height and distance apart of waves depends on:

- The strength of wind
- The length of time it has been blowing
- The fetch, which is the distance the wind has been blowing over the water
- The depth of water
- In the case of swell: the distance the waves have travelled.

WIND WAVES

Locally produced wind waves are generated very quickly, within an hour or so; and provided the wind is steady, the longer it blows the longer the wave length becomes. The wave front will often lie at an angle of a few degrees to the left of the wind direction, which will tend to make port tack a little faster than starboard. If the wind direction is changing, as with the sea breeze for instance, this angle between the wind and the wave front may be quite large. On the passage of a trough or front there will often be two distinct sets of waves, the angle between them being the difference in the wind angles either side of the trough. In the 1979 Fastnet storm the wave length was short both ahead of and behind the cold front, because the wind, though very strong, had been blowing for only a few hours. The resulting sea was notably confused.

The time taken for wind waves to decay depends on how long the wind that produced them was blowing. A fair rule of thumb is that the generation and decay times are similar.

If the wind is against the tide the wave length shortens, while it increases if the tide and wind are in the same direction. A strong current opposing a strong wind produces very steep and potentially dangerous waves especially in tidal races near headlands. Wind and tide in the same direction increase the wave length considerably and make for much easier sailing.

SWELL WAVES

The important swell waves are those that are generated over vast areas of open ocean. They contain a great deal of energy and take a long time (days) to decay. Swell waves always become steeper as they approach a shore, when the depth of water becomes less than one-twentieth of the wave length. This happens for wind waves as well, but not in water of sailing depth.

It is a useful fact that the longer swell waves travel faster than the shorter wind waves, so they can travel ahead and give advance warning of an approaching depression. Therefore the arrival or absence of swell provides a clear distinction between the advance of a local thunderstorm and an approaching depression. A threatening sky with increasing black clouds and rain cannot be part of an existing large wind system if there is no swell propagating forwards from it, so any wind will be temporary. On the other hand, increasing swell from the direction of advance of the storm clouds suggests an approaching depression with a large area of strong winds coming your way.

If there is swell which has been present for a long time without significant change the interpretation is doubtful; for instance the depression may be advancing, but very slowly.

SWELL WINDOWS

In many coastal areas, particularly among islands, it is important to be aware of swell windows. Sailing into a swell window you experience a sudden change from only locally generated wind waves to a mixture of wind waves and a much longer swell which may give a very uncomfortable roll and empty all the open lockers.

The best rule of thumb is that if between islands there is a deep water channel where you can 'see' the wind pointing at you from any distance away you must expect a swell. To provide passage for the swell the depth of water must

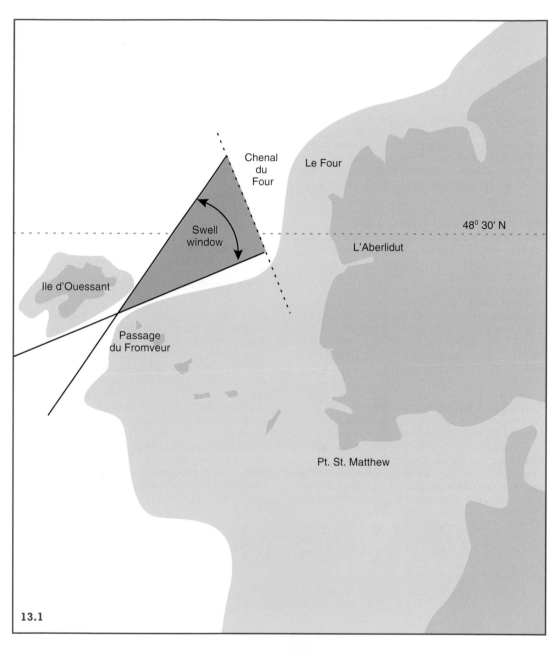

Chenal du Four

Le Four

Swell window

48° 30' N

L'Aberlidut

Ile d'Ouessant

Passage du Fromveur

Pt. St. Matthew

13.1

be at least one quarter of the distance between wave crests.

A good example of an ocean swell window is on passage through the Chenal du Four (figure 13.1). When the Passage du Fromeur and Le Four light are roughly abeam the window opens on some 3000 miles of uninterrupted ocean, and an Atlantic swell is often experienced, typically long and low, maybe 200 metres between crests.

FREAK WAVES

There really is no such thing as a freak wave. So many waves are generated in the sea and are continually combining together to form different sized waves, that statistically some are always bigger than others. The seventh wave is popularly supposed to be bigger than the other six. Similarly, there is the one in a hundred bigger still, the one in a thousand even bigger, and so on. Whether you sail the Channel, the

Bay of Biscay or the Atlantic you must expect to experience a wave bigger than the rest. The risk of being pooped or knocked onto your beam is always there, so be prepared.

WIND AND TIDE

A change of wind with a change of tide is not merely an old fisherman's tale. It really happens; not normally an abrupt change as the tide turns, but a gradual one over an hour or two as the wind adjusts to a new water temperature, shore temperature or drag.

Change in drag on the wind

This effect is easy to appreciate. When the tide is running with the wind the drag of the water on the wind is less than normal for a given wind strength, particularly since the sea would be relatively smooth and the length of waves relatively long. A tidal stream running against the wind involves a considerable increase in drag, due both to the change in relative speed and the increase in height and steepness of the waves. The actual windspeed then decreases and the direction backs a few degrees.

Change in water temperature

A change in tide is often accompanied by a change in water temperature, up or down depending upon whether the ebb or flood is from a warmer or colder source, or as a consequence of upwelling of colder water from beneath. Colder water leads to colder air near the sea surface, and thus increased stability and

a lighter, more backed wind at the sea surface for a given pressure gradient wind. Warmer water leads to warmer air near the sea surface, decreased stability and a stronger, more veered wind for a given pressure gradient.

So the clear message is: if you want the stronger and more veered wind, sail in the warmer water; if you want the lighter and more backed wind, sail in the colder water.

Change in shore temperature

The flooding by cold water of large areas of sun-heated mudflats or sand changes significantly (and often suddenly) the local sea-breeze generating forces. Consequent changes in wind speed and direction can be expected within two or three miles of the shore.

DANGEROUS WAVES

As we saw earlier, when it comes to the steepness of the waves, wind and tide are closely linked. Any change in wind or tide or both which involves the tide opposing the wind is potentially dangerous, and at best uncomfortable. Whenever the tide changes to run against the wind, or the wind changes to blow against the tide the distance apart of the waves is reduced, dramatically so when the stream is strong. This is discussed in more detail in Chapter 9 – Weather Hazards. Suffice it to say here that it is all too easy to think about changes in the tide, forgetting the wind, or to think about changes in the wind, forgetting the tide.

Opposite: The winds in this typhoon in the western Pacific reached over 140 knots.

14 Tropical cyclones

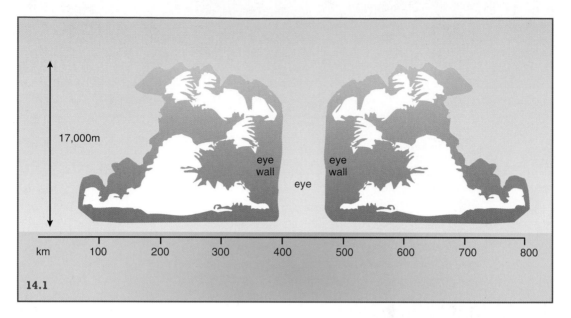

17,000m

eye
wall

eye
wall

eye

| km | 100 | 200 | 300 | 400 | 500 | 600 | 700 | 800 |

14.1

There is one kind of cyclone that derives virtually all its energy from the release of latent heat when condensation occurs. This is the tropical cyclone, otherwise known as a hurricane in the Atlantic, or typhoon in the Pacific.

These storms rely on the processes of evaporation and condensation. Evaporation takes water vapour and heat from the sea, while condensation releases them into the atmosphere. The necessary rate of evaporation occurs only when the sea temperature is high – at least 28^0 C. Such temperatures are experienced in the Atlantic only in the summer and early autumn, a period known in the Caribbean and Gulf of Mexico as 'the hurricane season'.

Tropical cyclones also need a little Coriolis force to start them spinning. So in their developing stage they are never nearer the equator than 7^0 N or 7^0 S. They usually start life as shallow depressions moving westwards south of the sub-tropical high, until they reach a suitably warm sea. As they spin, vast quantities of heat and water are released into the air and the typical 'warm core' develops with its characteristic cloud-free eye. Surrounding the eye is a solid wall of cloud extending upwards to over 15,000 metres (figure 14.1). Cooling by radiation from the top of the cloud increases the efficiency of this vast heat engine and the winds increase steadily, sometimes to over 150 knots. Avoiding a tropical cyclone is complicated by the fact that its track is often quite tortuous.

Only recently have computer models been developed which give reasonably reliable predictions. The best way to be sure of avoiding such storms is to stay away from seas where the temperature is 28^0 C or more. Figure 14.2 shows the average position of this isotherm in September.

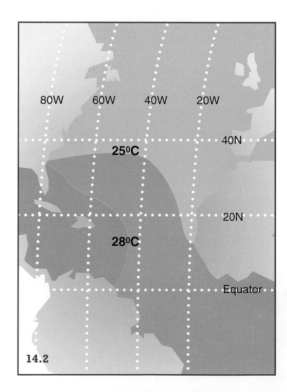

80W   60W   40W   20W

40N

25^0C

20N

28^0C

Equator

14.2

Much mariner's weather lore is useful and relates to the more frequently experienced sequences of wind, weather, cloud and pressure changes.

> When the wind backs and the
> weather glass falls,
> Then be on your guard against
> gales and squalls.

combines the signs of falling pressure and backing wind to provide a very reliable indication of the strong winds of an approaching depression. Looking at a backing wind only, the saying:

> When the wind goes against the sun,
> Trust it not for back `twill run.

provides only a note of caution.

The following saying is a good guide to the hurricane season in the Carribean:

> June – too soon;
> July – stand by;
> August – look out you must;
> September – remember;
> October – all over.

The following three sayings feature the sort of high clouds which typically precede a warm front or the trough of an approaching depression – particularly the long hair-like trails of cirrus, and sometimes cirrocumulus and altocumulus with its characteristic cellular structure.

> If clouds look as if scratched by a hen
> Get ready to reef your topsails then.

> Trace in the sky the painter's brush,
> Then winds around you soon will rush.

> Mackerel sky and mare's tails
> Make lofty ships carry low sails.

There are rules of thumb associated with the barometer:

> When the glass falls low,
> Prepare for a blow;
> When it rises high,
> Let all your kites fly.

is so obvious that it needs no further explanation. But two others related to pressure changes deserve comment:

First rise after low,
Foretells stronger blow.

describes what happens following some of the more vigorous cold fronts, when it is not unusual for the rise in pressure as the colder heavier air sweeps in to be so rapid that the pressure gradient increases dramatically. As a result the wind rises by two or three Beaufort forces for an hour or two.

Long foretold, long last,
Short notice soon past.

relates to the fact that major changes in the weather pattern are often preceded by several days of either falling or rising pressure, whereas rapid variations in pressure are characteristic of frequent and often rapid changes in the weather.

The ancient saying attributed to Virgil,

For ere the rising winds begin to roar,
The working seas advance
to wash the shore

is remarkable for its perception. In Chapter 13 we saw how swell waves travel relatively quickly and often give advance warning of an approaching depression with its strong winds.

Rain before seven
Fine before eleven.

merely highlights the fact that rain rarely lasts more than four hours at a time. It could equally read 'rain before eight, fine before twelve', or any other period of four hours in the day

Sky red in the morning,
Is a sailor's sure warning;
Sky red at night,
Is the sailor's delight.

is the sailor's version of the well-known shepherd's saying. It works on something like 60 per cent of occasions of a red sky, and is based on the observed sequence of events when the weather is moving from west to east – as is often the case. A red sky is seen in the morning when the rising sun illuminates cloud moving in from the west, typically with a front approaching. A red sky is seen in the evening when the setting sun illuminates cloud which is moving away eastwards followed by clearer weather from the west.

The following two sayings relate to the haloes which appear around the moon when it shines through a thin veil of cirrostratus, cloud which often precedes a warm front or trough; hence the reference to increasing wind.

If on her cheeks you see
the maiden's blush,
The ruddy moon foreshows
that winds will rush.

Weather foul expect when thou canst trace
A baleful halo circling Phoebus' face.

Another rhyme is worth remembering if only to scotch the often paraded idea that the moon is somehow responsible for changes in the weather. It is not. The reason for the misconception is the frequent change which both display, and the inevitable coincidences that arise.

The moon and the weather
May change together,
But change in the moon
Does not change the weather.
If we'd no moon at all,
And that may seem strange,
We still would have weather
That's subject to change.

16 Practical examples

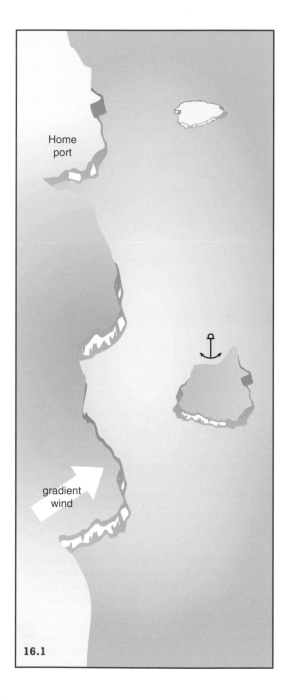

16.1

1. WHERE TO ANCHOR FOR LUNCH?

You have a day off. The tide is right for a day's sail starting early at about 0730. Your coast faces approximately east, and there are some pleasant coves and a couple of small islands (fig 16.1).

The shipping forecast indicates wind southwest force 3-4 with nothing said about it increasing or decreasing, and fair weather. Most coastal stations report for 0400 pressure 'falling slowly' or 'now falling', but the pressure is little different from that of the previous day, so the slowly falling pressure is nothing to worry about – the change is only diurnal. You notice a few clouds moving across from the southwest, which confirms the gradient wind inferred from the forecast. It is blowing offshore, and since you expect a fairly sunny day a good sea breeze is certain: starting fairly early from the east, slowly veering to SSE and probably not dying away till towards evening. So you decide that setting a course NNE would end up with a long, hard beat back to port. Instead you set course to the SE, making for the northwest-facing bay of a small island eight miles away. This will give a good anchorage for lunch, shelter from both the sea breeze and the sea-breeze chop, and confidence of a good wind home.

2. WET DAY DECISION

It is Thursday lunchtime in your office in Birmingham and pouring with rain outside. The weekend is not much more than 24 hours away and you want to try out your new Dory having just obtained your RYA Level 2 Powerboat qualification. The nearest coast is west Wales, but you also have the opportunity to visit a friend on the Thames estuary. The latest weather map in the newspaper shows a ridge of high pressure over northern Britain and an occlusion over southern England (figure 16.2). The shipping forecast until noon on Friday predicts easterly winds, Force 5 in Thames and Force 3 to 4 in the Irish Sea. You tap your barometer at home that evening and note a slight rise in pressure which seems hopeful, and you start

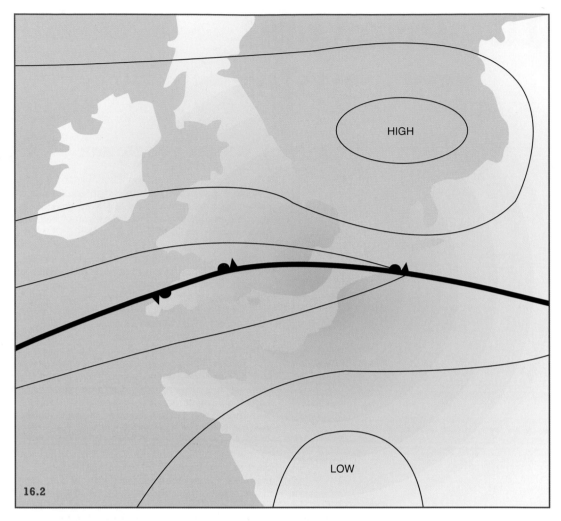

16.2

thinking seriously about going west. But you want to know for certain whether the wind will remain in the east.

The Metfax 2 and 3 day forecasts indicate a persistence of the ridge to the north with a slight movement south, consistent with the pressure trend on your barometer, and the weekend wind forecast for the Irish Sea continues the force 3 to 4 easterly. Rain is mentioned only for southern England. So you decide against the Thames estuary and head for the west Wales coast prepared to get on the water early on Saturday to take advantage of smooth water with the offshore wind and avoid rougher conditions with the likely afternoon sea breeze. Checking the tide tables you also figure that with the tide flooding in the morning and ebbing in the afternoon the river estuaries will be hazardous at both times with wind opposing tide.

So you launch your Dory on a stretch of west facing coast away from the rivers and enjoy a flat sea and little wind in the shelter of the mountains. As it turned out Saturday is cloudy and there is no sea breeze. Sunday is sunny with a light easterly in the morning and a fresh northwesterly sea breeze in the afternoon.

3. ACROSS THE CHANNEL AND BACK

Your weekend in Alderney has been planned for several weeks. You have studied the tides and decided on the best ETD to give you a favourable tide out of the Solent. Ideally you would like a wind on the beam for a fast reach both ways; for a crossing from the Needles this means either a northwesterly or a southeasterly. But as so often happens there is a seemingly endless sequence of depressions moving

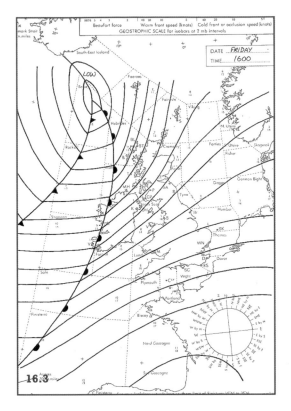

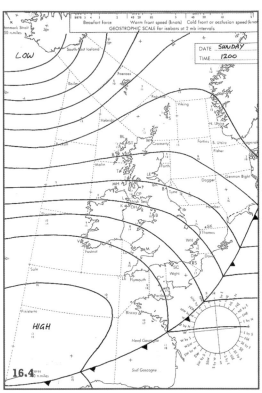

northeast between Scotland and Iceland, with their attendant fronts and intervening ridges moving east through the Channel.

On the Monday before you sail the 5 day forecast indicates the probability of a southerly, and you prepare yourself for a beat all the way, thankful that the strength is only 4 to 5. You follow the weather maps in the daily papers all week, and on Friday you pick up a more detailed map (figure 16.3). This bears out the earlier indications. The shipping forecast for sea area Wight is 'South to southwest 4 to 5 occasionally 6'. Referring to the map it is clear that the forecast direction – south to southwest – means southwesterly to start with, backing southerly as the warm front approaches, then veering southwesterly behind it. Judging from the distance apart of the isobars it looks as though the wind will be strongest just ahead of the front - which is where the 'occasionally force 6' comes in.

The spacing of the isobars along the warm front gives a warm front speed of about 15 knots (page 41), from which you deduce that it will be crossing Alderney at about mid-day on Saturday. So, realising that you will have a beat all the way, you decide to use the wind changes

to advantage by leaving the Needles on starboard tack while the wind is southwesterly and going about onto port as it backs towards southerly. You hope to make sufficient way to weather of Alderney to be able to close the island on starboard after the warm front has passed. You pay constant attention to the forecasts and to your barometer or barograph in case of unforeseen changes. The one remaining problem is the visibility and the probability of fog in the warm sector (between the warm and cold fronts).

The return trip on Sunday will be in the ridge behind the cold front (figure 16.4) The forecast is northwesterly 2 to 3 with good visibility. The weather map indicates a gradual backing in the wind, so you will be sailing freer as you cross. Closing the English coast after dusk will be complicated by the remains of the afternoon sea breeze – a calm patch, perhaps, and maybe an hour or two of southwesterly wind (See Chapter 11), details of which are never included in a shipping bulletin. With the forecast northwesterly gradient wind the night wind in the Solent is likely to be strongest near the island shore, whereas the afternoon sea breeze (southwesterly) will be strongest near the mainland shore.

Appendix 1
Coriolis force

If you have a sailor's appreciation of basic navigation skills you should find the following non-mathematical explanation of Coriolis force fairly easy to grasp. Let us visualise a spinning globe, see what the effects of the spin are at the pole and the equator, and then interpolate for the mid-latitudes.

The earth is spinning on an axis that passes through the north and south poles. If a mass of polar air moves away from the pole, it must be deflected because of the spin, whatever the direction it moves in. In practice air over the North Pole can only move south, and air over the South pole can only move north. And as it does so it is subject to an increase in the movement of the earth's surface beneath it. But this is only part of the story.

At the pole the spin axis is vertical to the earth's surface, which spins round it. The rate of spin is highest at this point, so Coriolis force is at a maximum. At the equator the spin axis is horizontal to the earth's surface, which moves around it like the rim of a wheel and does not spin at all – so the Coriolis force is zero.

Anywhere between the equator and the poles there will always be a component of the spin acting on moving air. It increases from zero at the equator to a maximum at the poles. This is the aspect most difficult to visualise. Try to imagine a three-dimensional spinning globe. If you stand a pencil over the pole it will be along the spin axis and you can visualise the pencil rotating and the earth spinning around it. Keeping the pencil vertical to the surface of the globe, slide it on its end until it reaches the equator. The component of spin about the axis of the pencil will gradually decrease until it becomes zero at the equator. It depends on the latitude. So wherever you are on the earth's surface – except at the equator – there is always a component of the earth's spin operating. The practical effect of this is to deflect sideways anything that moves freely – be it air or water, a golf ball or a bullet – and the deflection will operate regardless of the direction in which it is moving.

It is proverbially believed that bath water escaping down the plug hole is subject to Coriolis force and spins to the right in the northern hemisphere and to the left in the southern hemisphere. Not so! The fact is that for Coriolis force to be measurable the movement must cover a large area – a few kilometres at least – or last for an hour or two. The exit of the bath water is invariably determined by the way the plug is removed. Try it! Whether you are north or south of the equator you can get it spinning in either direction.

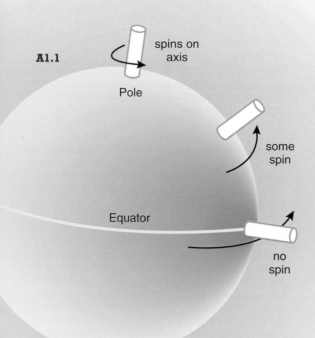

A1.1

spins on axis

Pole

some spin

Equator

no spin

At the equator, an object on the earth's surface travels fast but does not spin. At the pole it stays in one place but spins on its axis. If the object (or air mass) is moved away from the equator towards the pole the rate of horizontal movement decreases but the spin increases.

Appendix 2
The thermal wind

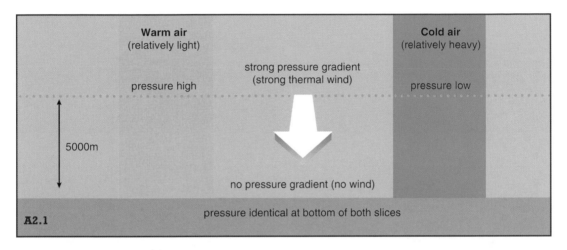

Warm air
(relatively light)

Cold air
(relatively heavy)

pressure high

strong pressure gradient
(strong thermal wind)

pressure low

5000m

no pressure gradient (no wind)

pressure identical at bottom of both slices

A2.1

Let's imagine vertical slices of warm and cold air some distance apart (figure A2.1), and assume that there is no pressure gradient at the ground and therefore no wind. Since pressure equates to weight, this means that the slice of warm air is the same weight as the slice of cold air.

Let's now go upwards through these slices to a typical height of altocumulus clouds, say 5000 metres. Since cold air is denser and therefore

heavier for the same depth than warm air, the decrease in pressure through the cold air will be greater than the decrease through the warm air. So as we rise there will be a steadily increasing pressure difference between the two slices. By the time we reach 5000 metres this pressure difference may be enough to give a wind of typically 50 to 100 knots; a wind entirely due to the temperature difference between the two slices of air. This is known as the thermal wind.

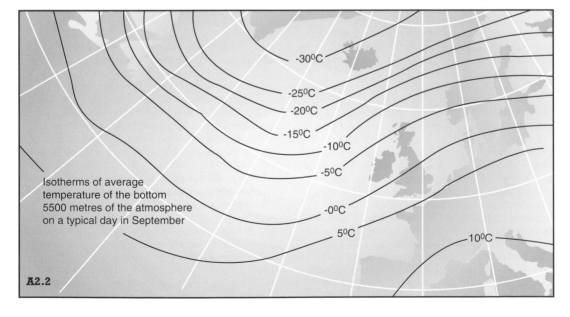

-30°C

-25°C

-20°C

-15°C

-10°C

-5°C

Isotherms of average
temperature of the bottom
5500 metres of the atmosphere
on a typical day in September

-0°C

5°C

10°C

A2.2

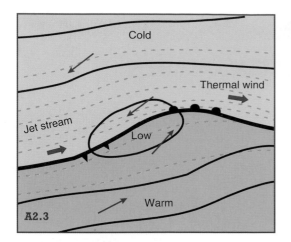

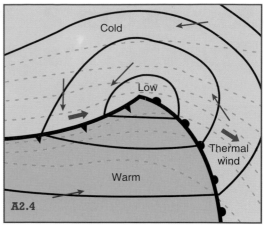

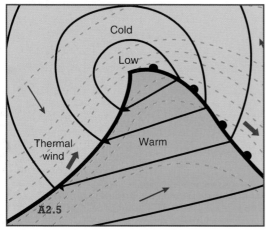

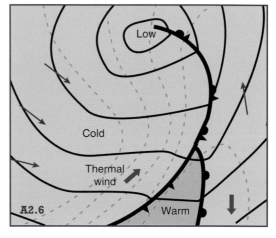

When there is a pressure gradient – and therefore wind – at the ground to start with, the wind component arising from the temperature difference between the two slices will be superimposed on the surface wind. In other words the thermal wind is the vector difference between the wind at any two heights and is directly related to the average horizontal temperature gradient in the air between those heights. The greater the temperature difference the stronger the wind.

In practice, wherever you are on the earth there is nearly always a temperature difference from place to place as areas of warmer or colder air move around, so there is nearly always a thermal wind with clouds moving at different speeds and in different directions at different heights. Figure A2.2 is a chart of isotherms of mean temperature for the bottom 5500 metres of the atmosphere for a day in September. A chart of the pressure difference between the surface and 5500 metres would have exactly the same shape, and the vector wind difference – which like all winds is subject to

Coriolis force – will blow parallel to the isobars (or isotherms).

Most of this may seem very theoretical, but one helpful practical application is the thermal equivalent of Buys Ballot's Law which states that if you stand with your back to the thermal wind the lower temperature will be to your left and the higher temperature to your right. So ahead of a warm front advancing from the west the isotherms will lie from approximately northwest to southeast and the thermal wind will be northwesterly, with warm air to the west (figure A2.4). The surface wind is likely to be southerly, but the cirrus and altostratus cloud will typically be seen streaming across from the northwest indicating a strong northwesterly thermal wind. The faster the clouds move the stronger the thermal wind and therefore the more vigorous the front is likely to be – a very useful warning of stormy weather to come. Similarly if you look back at the clouds following the passage of a vigorous cold front from west to east you will see them moving rapidly from a

Altostratus and altocumulus, typical of jet streams.

southwesterly direction, indicating colder air advancing from the west.

Figures A2.3 to A2.6 show the sequence of weather maps from Chapter 5 with the isotherms and thermal winds superimposed on them. Note how the isotherms are steadily distorted from the almost straight lines of figure A2.3 as cold air moves south behind the cold front and warm air pushes northeast in association with the warm front. As the low develops, the strong westerly winds aloft of figure A2.3 back steadily to southwesterly at the cold front and veer steadily to northwesterly at and ahead of the warm front.

JET STREAMS

The strongest upper level winds are known as jet streams. The title is usually reserved for winds in excess of 80 knots – winds of over 200 knots are not uncommon. They are found where the isotherms are closest together, either along the polar front, or at the warm and cold fronts of a depression (which are distortions of the polar front) at heights between 5000 and 10,000 metres.

Occasionally you may see an almost stationary band of upper cloud – usually altocumulus or cirrocumulus – with the clouds moving rapidly along the line of the band. This is evidence of the jet stream (figure A2.3). Subsequent movement of the band will indicate the sort of weather to come. If the cloud edge is advancing with the upper wind well veered from the surface wind, the weather will deteriorate; if the cloud edge is receding with the upper wind backed from the surface wind, the weather will improve.

Appendix 3
DIY - Your own weather map

There is a great deal more to be gleaned from a shipping bulletin than simply the forecast of wind speed and direction for the particular area in which you are sailing. The information for all the other areas, together with the latest observations from a selection of coastguard stations, lighthouses, lightvessels and buoys, is sufficient to reconstruct the weather map for the whole area over and around the British Isles, thus setting the forecast for your area in context, and providing a basis for judging variations in the wind and weather which may affect your passage.

A forecaster when writing the forecast for shipping will consult two weather maps; one called an 'actual' for the latest main observing time available (0000, 0600, 1200,1800 GMT) and the other a forecast chart for 24 hours later than this time. The 'general synopsis' describes briefly the important features of these charts, and the forecast which is given for sea areas all around the country is a synthesis of what these two chart show, starting with what the weather is now through to what is expected in 24 hours time. You can with a little practice reverse this procedure, and working backward from the forecast reconstruct the essential parts of both the charts the forecaster started with.

The easiest and most useful application of the shipping bulletin, however, is to construct a single weather map for the time for which the observations are given, i.e. a time *between* the times of the two maps used by the forecaster. For instance, for the early morning shipping bulletin the forecaster will be looking at an actual chart for midnight GMT and a forecast chart for the following midnight. The observations given in the bulletin will be for 0400. So you can construct a chart for 0400 using the observations and interpolating for this time the position of the weather systems and the strength and direction of the winds from the forecast.

The following paragraphs describe the process of transcribing the shipping bulletin and drawing a weather map for all or part of the area covered. The only bit of theory you need to know is that there is a relationship between the pressure pattern and the wind, and that the surface wind over the sea blows slightly across the isobars towards low pressure.

Abridged Beaufort weather notation and international plotting symbols

Weather	Beaufort letter	plotting symbol
rain	r	●
drizzle	d	,
snow	s	✳
shower	p	▽
hail	h	△
thunderstorm	th	↰
squall	q	▽
mist	m	═
fog	f	≡
haze	z	∞

TRANSCRIBING THE SHIPPING BULLETIN

Have a pre-prepared form to hand. The Metmap published jointly by the Royal Meteorological Society and the RYA is recommended and is used here. You will also need some easily recognised abbreviations and shorthand. The following are well tried and tested and incorporate some used professionally. Familiarity with them will have the double benefit of enabling you to appreciate at a glance information provided on fax broadcasts and displayed at ports of call.

The general synopsis

Few international symbols are involved here except for the points of the compass – N, S, NW, SW etc. Initial letters are the best shorthand for weather systems – L for low, H for high and so on. One very useful hint is to use a vertical stroke or solidus to denote the passage of time. Movement is best denoted by an arrow. Thus 'a depression 996 mb over Faeroes at 1200 today is expected over German Bight 978 mb by 1200 tomorrow' is written as 'L 996 Faer/ 978 G Bt'.

Sea area forecasts

Winds are always transcribed in terms of points of the compass and force, and using the solidus for the passage of time, a sentence such as 'northwest 4 to 5 at first backing south-west and increasing to 7 to gale 8 by the end of the period' is written simply as 'NW 4-5/SW 7-8'. Similarly 'in the South at first' is written 'in S/' and 'in the north later' as '/in N'.

Weather

This is always given in terms such as 'fair', 'showers', 'rain', etc. Here international shorthand should be used and you can choose between the Beaufort letter notation or the international weather map symbols as given opposite. There is something to be said for using the international map symbols because you can then plot these directly on to your map, but the former are much easier to learn and you can readily turn them into plotting symbols at your leisure after the broadcast. The phrases 'at first', and 'later', are often used and, again, a vertical stroke or solidus comes in very useful. For instance 'rain at first, showers later', can be abbreviated to 'r/p'. This sort of detail should always be taken down as it almost certainly ties in with a change of wind and the passage of an important weather system through the sea area.

For heavy precipitation, capital letters are used, e.g. R - heavy rain.

Visibility

A straightforward abbreviation of 'g' for 'good', 'm' for 'moderate' and 'p' for 'poor' is all that is required here, remembering again to use a vertical stroke to denote passage of time and also to take down all the details which are given about fog.

Coastal station reports

As with the sea area forecasts you need a prepared form with the coastal stations already listed, and columns for the reports which are always given for each station in the following sequence:

- wind
- significant weather – not yet included in reports from automatic stations. (Fair and fine are not 'significant' and are not mentioned.)
- visibility in miles or metres
- barometric pressure in millibars
- pressure tendency (i.e. whether the barometer is rising or falling and how rapidly).

The same shorthand should be used as for the sea area forecasts. There is no need to write down the words 'miles' or 'metres' as one- or two-digit figures will always be metres. Writing down the value of pressure it saves time to use only the last two digits – anything over 50 will normally be 9–, and anything under 50 will be 10--. The pressure tendency should be abbreviated with the initial letters, or you can use a stroke inclined at various angles according to the way you would observe the movement of pressure on a barograph.

PLOTTING A WEATHER MAP

Having taken down the information, your next step is to plot it on a weather chart. Throughout the world there is a standard format for doing this. The wind is always drawn as a feathered arrow blowing towards the observing position and with the 'feathers' always on the clockwise side of the arrow. The number of feathers is always proportional to the wind strength. For winds given in Beaufort force use one feather for force 2, one and a half for force 3 and so on. The rest of the information is accommodated around the observing position like this:

visibility weather   **pressure**
pressure tendency

So northwest 5, continuous slight rain, 2 miles, 1009 millibars, falling is plotted like this:

09

2 ••

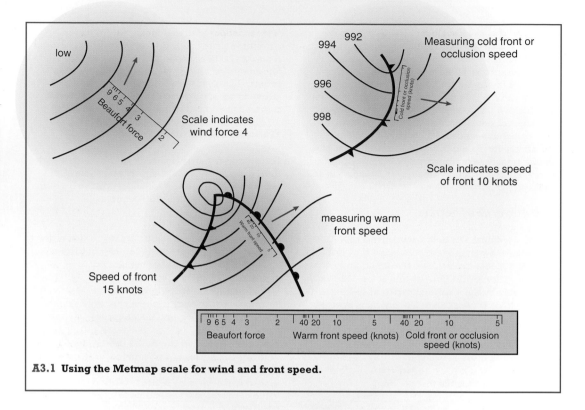

A3.1 Using the Metmap scale for wind and front speed.

Similarly plot the wind and the weather in each one of the sea areas, using more than one plot as necessary depending on the amount of information given. For instance a forecast for sea area Forties of 'northwest 4 to 5 in east, 6 to 7 in west, showers, good' is plotted:

It is best to plot the average or highest value, but remember that you have done so when fitting the isobars. Make sure you also write down somewhere on the chart the time at which the observations were made. Include your own observation as well.

Finally plot the positions of highs and lows and their pressure values from the general synopsis. Also sketch in the positions of troughs and ridges if any are given. Note that you are reconstructing a weather map for the time at which the observations were made at the coastal stations. This means interpolating the values and positions of the highs, lows, fronts, etc., between the start time in the general synopsis - usually 4 to 5 hours earlier - and the end time, which is usually 19 or 20 hours later than the time of the observations.

CONSTRUCTING YOUR OWN WEATHER MAP

Do not start drawing your weather map until you have some idea of what shape it should be. Always refer back to the most recent available chart; the one you drew yourself or the one in the newspaper. Starting from scratch is very difficult, even for a professional meteorologist.

Drawing the isobars

The next step is to establish the general shape of the pressure pattern using the observations of pressure and wind. In my experience it is best to use feathery pencil lines to sketch the approximate positions of the isobars, making some lines darker than others as you approach the solution. Do not be put off by the skill and precision with which some charts are drawn. Your solution is likely to be just as useful.

We know that the pressure gradient, which on a weather map is given by the distance apart of the isobars, is inversely proportional to the wind speed. A scale relating wind speed to the distance apart of the isobars can be used either to derive the wind speed from isobars already drawn, or, given the wind speed, to draw the isobars the right distance apart. The scale must be related to the distance scale appropriate to the map projection. Most charts used for drawing weather maps have a scale printed in one corner. The example in figure A3.1 is taken from the Metmap.

The relationship between pressure gradient and surface wind speed is slightly dependent on latitude and the curvature of the isobars, and also on whether the air is stable or unstable. The scale on the Metmap assumes straight isobars over a sea surface and marginally unstable conditions. It is reasonably valid between 40 degrees N and 60 degrees N. Allow for lighter winds than prescribed in higher latitudes, in strongly curved isobars around a low and also in stable conditions. Allow for stronger winds than prescribed in lower latitudes in strongly curved isobars around a high and in unstable conditions.

Don't forget that wind directions and strengths reported from coastal stations may be influenced by local coastal effects and sea or land breezes, so that they may not fit the isobars. You will have to work it out. Winds from lightvessels far from land are more reliable.

So, referring if possible to a previous weather map, either in the newspaper or one you drew yourself, draw the new positions of the isobars starting where you have observed pressure values and then extending outwards to the known positions of centres of low and high pressure, all the time using your dividers to get the isobars approximately the right distance apart according to the scale. Over sea areas the isobars should be aligned to the wind so that it is blowing almost parallel to them but slightly towards low pressure. Keep to standard values for the isobars, usually every 4 mb up or down from 1000 mb, or in light winds every 2 mb, and remember that reported pressure values are rounded up or down to the nearest mb, so you have a bit of latitude in where to put the lines.

Drawing the fronts and troughs

Here considerations of continuity are particularly useful. Where was the front 24 or 12 hours ago? What position, if any, was given in the shipping bulletin? What is the wind component at right angles to it? How far is it likely to have moved from its last known position up to the time for which you are constructing the chart? Is this compatible with the forecast position?

The scale you use for relating the wind speed to the distance apart of the isobars can be adapted to measure the speed of a front or trough. The instantaneous speed of these features is proportional to the wind component at right angles to their line of advance. Cold fronts and typical troughs in cold air move relatively faster than warm fronts. A scale is provided in the corner of the Metmap and figure A3.1 shows how to use it.

The latest observations are also important. Do the differences in wind direction, weather, and pressure tendency between one side of the front (trough) and the other support your analysis? The table will remind you of the typical changes at a front or trough.

	Trough	Warm front	Cold front
wind	veers	veers	veers
visibility	–	decreases	increases
weather	clearance after rain	drizzle or fair after rain	clearance after rain
pressure	rise after fall	steady after fall	rise after fall

Finally, having determined the position of the trough or front, identify it with the standard symbols: a dotted line for a trough, and for a front a solid line with blobs or spikes protruding from its leading edge depending on whether it is a warm or cold front.

You will then need to redraw the isobars at the fronts so that they show a clear discontinuity. Indeed you will often wish to sketch in the positions of fronts and troughs before you start drawing the isobars.

USING YOUR WEATHER MAP

Having drawn your weather map you will have a very much better understanding of the weather situation and a much better ability to interpret the naked forecast than if you had just written down the forecasts for your sea area. For instance, the forecast wind may be southwesterly force 5. It may be critical for a long beat to windward to know whether 'southwesterly' means 220 degrees or 240 degrees. Your map will help you decide. It will also indicate whether force 6 is more likely over one side of the sea area than the other, or later rather than sooner. When the direction is given as 'south-west to west' your map may reveal a bend in the isobars with west at one side of the area and southwest at the other; or alternatively it may reveal a weak trough which you can expect to be moving through the area. A multitude of minor inferences are possible which taken over a season make your sailing safer, more skilful and more enjoyable.

Two examples follow of actual shipping bulletins transcribed and turned into weather maps.

**AND NOW THE SHIPPING FORECAST
ISSUED BY THE METEORLOGICAL OFFICE
AT 1705 ON SUNDAY 27TH MARCH**

GALE WARNINGS ARE IN OPERATION FOR SEA
AREAS FINISTERRE, SOLE AND ROCKALL

THE GENERAL SYNOPSIS AT 1200
LOW FINISTERRE 996 MOVING NORTHEAST
TO SOUTH NORWAY 995 BY THE SAME TIME
TOMORROW. LOW HEBRIDES 995 EXPECTED
400 MILES NORTH OF VIKING 978 BY THE
SAME TIME

**THE AREA FORECASTS FOR THE
NEXT 24 HOURS**
VIKING, NORTH UTSIRE, SOUTH UTSIRE, FORTIES
SOUTHERLY VEERING WESTERLY 5 TO 6, RAIN
MOVING EAST THEN SHOWERS, MODERATE
WITH FOG PATCHES BECOMING GOOD
CROMARTY, FORTH
SOUTHERLY 4 TO 5 VEERING WESTERLY AND
INCREASING 7, RAIN THEN SHOWERS,
MODERATE OR POOR BECOMING GOOD
TYNE, DOGGER, FISHER, GERMAN BIGHT
SOUTHERLY 5 TO 7 VEERING NORTHWEST
LATER, RAIN LATER, MODERATE WITH FOG
PATCHES, BECOMING GOOD
HUMBER, THAMES, DOVER
SOUTHERLY 4 TO 5 VEERING NORTHWEST 7,
RAIN LATER, MODERATE OR GOOD BUT POOR
FOR A TIME
WIGHT, PORTLAND, PLYMOUTH
SOUTHERLY VEERING NORTHWESTERLY 4 TO 5
INCREASING 7 FOR A TIME, RAIN OR
SHOWERS BECOMING FAIR, GOOD BUT
POOR FOR A TIME
BISCAY
SOUTHEASTERLY BECOMING NORTHERLY, 4
TO 5 INCREASING 7, RAIN AT TIMES,
MODERATE LOCALLY POOR AT FIRST
FINISTERRE, SOLE
NORTHWEST 6 TO 8 BUT SOUTHERLY 5 TO 7
IN EAST AT FIRST, RAIN AT TIMES, MODERATE
OR POOR
LUNDY, FASTNET, IRISH SEA
SOUTHERLY VEERING NORTHWESTERLY 4 TO 5
BUT INCREASING 7 FOR A TIME, RAIN THEN
FAIR, MODERATE OCCASIONALLY POOR
BECOMING GOOD
SHANNON
NORTHWEST 5 BECOMING SOUTHERLY 6
TO GALE 8, SHOWERS THEN RAIN, GOOD
BECOMING MODERATE

ROCKALL
WEST 6 INCREASING GALE 8 FOR A TIME
BACKING SOUTHERLY LATER, SHOWERS,
MAINLY GOOD
MALIN, HEBRIDES, BAILEY, FAIR ISLE
SOUTHWEST 5 VEERING WESTERLY 6 TO GALE
8, RAIN THEN SHOWERS, MODERATE OR POOR
BECOMING GOOD
FAEROES
CYCLONIC 5 BECOMING WESTERLY 5 TO 7,
SHOWERS, MODERATE BECOMING GOOD
SOUTHEAST ICELAND
CYCLONIC 4 BECOMING NORTHWEST 5, RAIN
OR SHOWERS, GOOD

**WEATHER REPORTS FROM
COASTAL STATIONS FOR 1600**
TIREE
WEST FOUR, 19 MILES, 1002, RISING
BUTT OF LEWIS
SOUTH SOUTH WEST 6, INTERMITTENT, SLIGHT
RAIN, 11 MILES, 997, FALLING MORE SLOWLY
SUMBURGH
SOUTH SOUTH EAST 4, HAZE, 2 MILES, 1001,
FALLING
ST ABBS HEAD
SOUTHWEST 5, HAZE, 2 MILES, 1004,
NOW RISING
SMITHS KNOLL AUTOMATIC
SOUTHEAST 3, 5 MILES, 1008, STEADY
DOVER
SOUTHWEST 3, 5 MILES, 1008,
FALLING SLOWLY
ROYAL SOVEREIGN
SOUTHWEST BY SOUTH 4, 5 MILES, 1008,
FALLING SLOWLY
CHANNEL LIGHT VESSEL AUTOMATIC
SOUTHWEST 1, 11 MILES, 1007,
RISING SLOWLY
LANDS END
EAST SOUTH EAST 4, MIST, 1 MILE, 1005,
FALLING
VALENTIA
NORTH 3, INTERMITTENT SLIGHT RAIN,
6 MILES, 1006, RISING SLOWLY
RONALDSWAY
SOUTH BY WEST 4, SMOKE, 3 MILES, 1005,
NOW FALLING
MALIN HEAD
WEST BY SOUTH 4, INTERMITTENT SLIGHT
RAIN, 16 MILES, 1003, RISING
JERSEY
SOUTHEAST BY SOUTH 3, 16 MILES, 1007,
FALLING MORE SLOWLY.

AND NOW THE SHIPPING FORECAST ISSUED BY THE METEOROLOGICAL OFFICE AT 1705 ON MONDAY 28TH MARCH

GALE WARNINGS ARE IN OPERATION FOR SEA AREAS FINISTERRE, SOLE, SHANNON, ROCKALL, MALIN, HEBRIDES, BAILEY, FAIR ISLE, SOUTHEAST ICELAND

THE GENERAL SYNOPSIS AT 1200
ATLANTIC LOW MOVING NORTHEAST EXPECTED 200 MILES WEST OF ROCKALL 978 BY THE SAME TIME TOMORROW

THE AREA FORECAST FOR THE NEXT 24 HOURS
VIKING
WEST 5 BACKING SOUTH AND INCREASING 6 TO GALE 8, SHOWERS, MODERATE OR GOOD
NORTH UTSIRE, SOUTH UTSIRE,
WEST BACKING SOUTH 4 TO 5, SHOWERS, MODERATE OR GOOD
FORTIES, CROMARTY, FORTH
SOUTHWEST BACKING 4 TO 5 OCCASIONALLY 6, LOCALLY GALE 8 LATER, SHOWERS AT FIRST, MODERATE OR GOOD
TYNE, DOGGER
NORTHWESTERLY BACKING SOUTHERLY 4 TO 5, SHOWERS AT FIRST, MODERATE OR GOOD
FISHER, GERMAN BIGHT
WEST TO NORTHWEST 4 TO 5 BECOMING VARIABLE 3, SHOWERS AT FIRST, MODERATE BECOMING GOOD
HUMBER, THAMES
NORTHWESTERLY 5 BACKING SOUTHERLY AND DECREASING 3 TO 4, SHOWERS AT FIRST, MODERATE BECOMING GOOD
DOVER, WIGHT, PORTLAND
CYCLONIC 3 TO 4, SHOWERS, MODERATE OR GOOD
PLYMOUTH
NORTHERLY 5 TO 6 BACKING SOUTHWESTERLY AND DECREASING 3 TO 4, MAINLY FAIR, MODERATE OR GOOD
BISCAY
VARIABLE 3 BECOMING NORTHERLY 5 IN WEST, MAINLY FAIR, MODERATE OR GOOD
FINISTERRE
NORTHERLY 6 TO 7 LOCALLY GALE 8 AT FIRST DECREASING 5 LATER, MAINLY FAIR, GOOD
SOLE
NORTHERLY 6 TO GALE 8 BACKING SOUTHERLY AND DECREASING 5, RAIN AT TIMES, GOOD BECOMING MODERATE
LUNDY, FASTNET
NORTHERLY BACKING SOUTHWESTERLY 5 TO 6 DECREASING 4 FOR A TIME, MAINLY FAIR, MAINLY GOOD

IRISH SEA
NORTHERLY 4 BACKING SOUTH TO SOUTHWESTERLY INCREASING 5 TO 6, FAIR, MAINLY GOOD
SHANNON, ROCKALL
SOUTHERLY 5 INCREASING 6 TO GALE 8 OCCASIONALLY SEVERE GALE 9, RAIN OR SHOWERS, GOOD BECOMING MODERATE OR POOR
MALIN, HEBRIDES
WESTERLY 4 TO 5 LOCALLY 7 AT FIRST, BACKING SOUTHERLY AND INCREASING 6 TO GALE 8, RAIN LATER, GOOD BECOMING MODERATE
BAILEY
WESTERLY 4 TO 5 BACKING SOUTH TO SOUTHEASTERLY 6 TO GALE 8 OCCASIONALLY SEVERE GALE 9, RAIN LATER, GOOD BECOMING MODERATE
FAIR ISLE, FAEROES, SOUTH EAST ICELAND
WESTERLY 5 TO 7 DECREASING 4 THEN BACKING SOUTH TO SOUTHEASTERLY AND INCREASING GALE FORCE 8, SHOWERS AT FIRST THEN RAIN, GOOD BECOMING MODERATE

WEATHER REPORTS FROM COASTAL STATIONS FOR 1600
TIREE
WEST BY NORTH FIVE, 27 MILES, 1015, RISING
BUTT OF LEWIS
WEST BY SOUTH SEVEN, PRECIPITATION WITHIN SIGHT, 11 MILES, 1010 RISING
SUMBURGH
WESTSOUTHWEST FIVE, PRECIPITATION WITHIN SIGHT, 19 MILES, 1005, RISING MORE SLOWLY
ST ABBS HEAD
WEST BY NORTH SIX, 22 MILES, 1014, RISING
SMITHS KNOLL AUTOMATIC
NORTH SIX, 11 MILES, 1012, RISING
DOVER
WESTSOUTHWEST TWO, 5 MILES, 1013, RISING
ROYAL SOVEREIGN
SOUTH WEST FOUR, 5 MILES, 1014, RISING
CHANNEL LIGHT VESSEL AUTOMATIC
WESTNORTHWEST TWO, 5 MILES, 1015, RISING
LANDS END
NORTH BY EAST SEVEN, 13 MILES, 1016, RISING
VALENTIA
WEST BY NORTH THREE, 22 MILES, 1020, RISING MORE SLOWLY
RONALDSWAY
NORTH BY WEST FOUR, MORE THAN 38 MILES, 1018, RISING MORE SLOWLY
MALIN HEAD
WEST FOUR, 22 MILES, 1017, RISING
JERSEY
WEST BY NORTH TWO, 7 MILES, 1015, RISING

R. MET. SOC./R.Y.A. METMAP — at 1200, 28 MARCH

GENERAL SYNOPSIS: At L → NE → 200 m W of R 978

Gales	SEA AREA FORECAST	Wind	Weather	Visibility
	Viking	WS 6-8	▽	m or g
	N. Utsire	W/S 4-5	▽	m or g
	S. Utsire			
	Forties			
	Cromarty	W/S 4-5 occ 6 / 8	▽	m g
	Forth			
	Tyne	NWJ/S 4-5	◖|	m g
	Dogger			
	Fisher	W-NW 4-5 / V 3	▽|	m / g
	German Bight			
	Humber	NWS / S 3-4	▽|	m / g
	Thames			
	Dover			
	Wight	cyc 3-4	▽	mg
	Portland			
	Plymouth	N 5-6 / SW 3-4	mf	mg
	Biscay	V3 / N in W	mf	mg
X	Finisterre			
X	Sole	N 6-7 loc 8 / 5	mf	g / m
	Lundy	N / SW 5-6 / 4	•	mg
	Fastnet	N4 / S-SW 5-6	f	mg / m p
X	Shannon	S5 / 6-8 occ 9	•▽	g / m p
X	Rockall			
X	Malin	W 4-5 loc 7 / S 6-8	•	g / m
X	Hebrides			
X	Bailey	W 4-5 / S-SE 6-8 occ 9	•	g / m
X	Fair Isle			
X	Faeroes	W S-7 / 4 / S-SE 8	▽•	g / m
X	SE Iceland			

COASTAL REPORTS (Shipping Bulletin) at 1600 BST

	Wind Direction	Force	Weather	Visibility	Pressure	Trend
Tiree	W/S	7	⊙	27	15	r
Butt of Lewis	WSW	5	⊙	11	10	r
Sumburgh	W/N	6	⊙	19	05	rms
St Abb's Head	N	6		22	14	r
Smiths Knoll Auto	N	3		11	12	r
Dover	S/SW	4		5	13	r
Royal Sovereign	SW	2		13	14	r
Channel L.V. Auto	NNW	2		5	15	r
Land's End	N/E	3		13	16	r
Valentia	W/N	3		22	20	rms
Ronaldsway	NW/W	4		>38	18	rms
Malin Head	W	4		22	17	r
Jersey	W/N	2		7	15	r

COASTAL REPORTS (Inshore Waters) at .... BST/GMT

Boulmer						
Bridlington						
Walton on the Naze						
St Catherine's Point						
Land's End						
Mumbles						
Valley						
Blackpool						
Ronaldsway						
Killough						
Orlock Head						
Larne						
Corsewall Point						
Prestwick						
Benbecula						
Stornoway						
Lerwick						
Wick						
Aberdeen						
Leuchars						

7/90

R. MET. SOC./R.Y.A. METMAP — at 1200, 27 MARCH

GENERAL SYNOPSIS:
L Fin → NE S Nor 995
L Heb → 400 m N of Vik 978

Gales	SEA AREA FORECAST	Wind	Weather	Visibility
	Viking	S/W 5-6	•	
	N. Utsire		→ E / ▽	m ☰ g
	S. Utsire			
	Forties			
	Cromarty	S 4-5 / W7	• / ▽	m p / g
	Forth			
	Tyne	S 5-7 / NW	•|	m ☰ g
	Dogger			
	Fisher			
	German Bight			
	Humber	S 4-5 / NW7	•|	mg / pl
	Thames			
	Dover			
	Wight	S / NW 4-5 → 7	• or ▽ / f	g / pl
	Portland			
	Plymouth	SE/N 4-5 / 7	•	m loc P
	Biscay			
X	Finisterre			
X	Sole	NW 6-8 / S 5-7 in E	•	m / p
	Lundy			
	Fastnet	S / NW 4-5 / 7	•|	m occ p / g
	Irish Sea			
	Shannon	NWS / S 6-8 / 5	▽ •	g / m
X	Rockall	W6/8 / 5	▽	mg
	Malin			
	Hebrides	SWS / W6-8	• ▽	m p / g
	Bailey			
	Fair Isle			
	Faeroes	cyc 5 / W 5-7	▽	m / g
	SE Iceland	cyc 4 / NW 5	• ▽	g

COASTAL REPORTS (Shipping Bulletin) at 1600 BST

	Wind Direction	Force	Weather	Visibility	Pressure	Trend
Tiree	W	4		19	02	r
Butt of Lewis	SSW	4	•	11	97	fms
Sumburgh	SSE	4	h	2	01	f
St Abb's Head	SE	5	h	5	04	r
Smiths Knoll Auto	SE	3		5	08	s
Dover	SW	3		5	08	fs
Royal Sovereign	SWS	4		5	08	fs
Channel L.V. Auto	SW	1		11	04	rs
Land's End	ESE	4	m	6	06	f
Valentia	S/W	4	s	3	05	nf
Ronaldsway	N/S	4	•	16	03	r
Malin Head	SE/S	3		16	07	fms
Jersey						

COASTAL REPORTS (Inshore Waters) at .... BST/GMT

Boulmer						
Bridlington						
Walton on the Naze						
St Catherine's Point						
Land's End						
Mumbles						
Valley						
Blackpool						
Ronaldsway						
Killough						
Orlock Head						
Larne						
Corsewall Point						
Prestwick						
Berbecula						
Stornoway						
Lerwick						
Wick						
Aberdeen						
Leuchars						

7/90

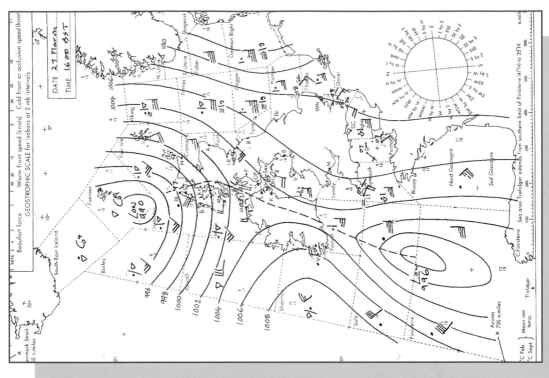

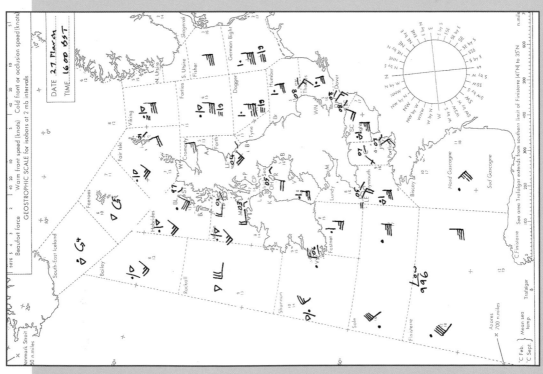

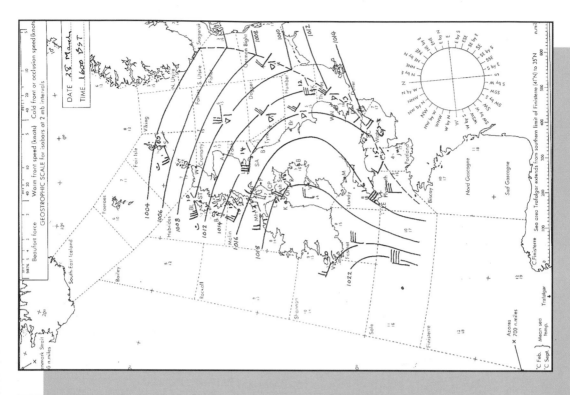

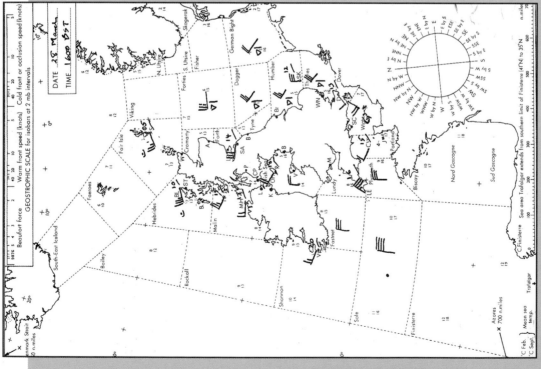

Appendix 4
UK sea areas

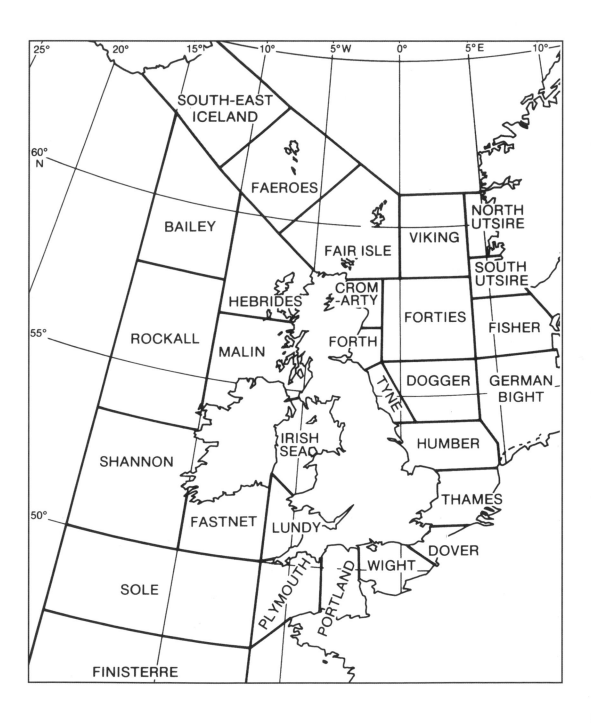

Index

Air mass	6	Lee low	27
Alto-	18	*Levanter*	49
Anticylone	9	*Leveche*	49
		Low	9
Backing	13		
Beaufort Force	34	Metres per second	33
Beaufort letters	70	Millibar	9
Bora	49	*Mistral*	49
Buys Ballot's Law	13		
		Navtex	32
Chili	49	Nimbus	18
Clouds	4, 17	Nimbostratus	18
Cloud streets	21		
Cirrus, cirro-	18	Occlusion	25, 29
Col	9		
Cold front	12, 28	Polar front	24
Coriolis Force	9, 66	Polar low	27
Cumulonimbus	18	Pressure	9
Cumulus	18	Pressure gradient wind	9
Cyclone	9	Pressure tendency	35
Depression	9	Ridge	9
Dewpoint	44		
Doldrums	7	*Scirocco*	49
		Sea areas	79
Etesian	49	Sea breeze	50
		Sea state	36
Fog	4, 43	Soon	35
Föhn	49	Squall	43
Front	12, 28, 29	Stable	14
Front speed	41	Stratocumulus	18
Front symbols	12	Stratus	18
		Subsiding	6
Gale	33	Surface wind	14
Geostrophic scale	10, 11	Swell	56
Ghibli	49	Synoptic chart	12
Gradient wind	9		
Gregale	49	Thunderstorm	43
		Trade winds	6, 7, 54
Heat low	27	Trade wind cumulus	54
Hectopascal	9	*Tramontana*	49
High	9	Trough	9
Holes in the wind	38	Typhoon	60
Hurricane	60		
		Unstable	14
Imminent	35		
Isobar	9	Veering	13
		Vendeval	49
Jet stream	7, 69	*Verdarro*	49
		Visibility	35
Khamsin	49	Vortex rolls	54
Knot	33		
		Warm front	12, 28, 29
Land breeze	48	Weight of wind	15
Latent heat	6	Wind waves	56
Later	35		